BAFFLED
BY BALANCE
SHEETS?

BAFFLED BY BALANCE SHEETS?

How to Understand Company Accounts
Quickly and Easily

William Lee Johnson

Kogan Page

First published in Zimbabwe in 1987 by Keppel Publishers.

This totally revised and rewritten edition published in Great Britain in 1988
by Kogan Page Limited, 120 Pentonville Road, London N1 9JN.

British Library Cataloguing in Publication Data

Johnson, W. L. (William Lee)
Baffled by balance sheets?
1. Balance sheets. Interpretation
I. Title
657'.33

ISBN 1-85091-536-9
ISBN 1-85091-537-7 Pbk

Printed and bound in Great Britain by
Biddles Ltd, Guildford

Contents

Appendices

Preface

The object of this book is to teach the reader how to read a balance sheet, and to give an insight into business finance generally.

Business finance is a fascinating subject, and knowledge of the subject is useful, indeed valuable, in just about every job in business, industry, and administration and particularly if you are running your own business.

Baffled by Balance Sheets? is not a textbook, so it does not cover every nuance and detail of accounting. But accountancy students will find it a useful introduction to their studies.

The book is based on a course I have presented often over the past 15 years. Most of the men and women attending have been managers, business people, professionals, sales people – practical, busy people – but few have been academically inclined. So the course, and this book, are presented in a non-academic way. It uses the everyday experiences of men and women as much as possible. It teaches the subject step by step. Vocabulary is carefully introduced. But at the same time, the book does not shy away from difficult topics.

At the end of most chapters a self-check questionnaire has been included. These self-checks are important because they will highlight important points which might otherwise have been missed or misunderstood. Also, the questionnaires amount to a summary and revision of the chapter, and this helps long-term memory. So readers are urged to do all these tests.

Baffled by Balance Sheets? is written without the balance sheets and business finance of any one country in mind. It covers both the United Kingdom and the Commonwealth countries, which have inherited the British approach to company law and balance sheets.

A glance through the Glossary will act as a quick revision when the reader has completed the book.

William Lee Johnson

Chapter 1
The Shape of a Balance Sheet

Liabilities and assets

All of us are worth something. The question is, how much?

To find out how much you are worth, you must first decide how much each of your *assets* is worth. Your assets are things like your car, or your watch – anything you can turn into cash. £500 owing to you by your son-in-law is also an asset – one day it will become cash. Add up your assets.

Then add up your *liabilities*.

Your liabilities are the things you owe *now*, like the money you owe your dentist for the work he did last week. The balance of the mortgage loan you owe to the building society is also a liability – even though you have 20 years in which to repay it. Money you will owe for something which will happen *in the future* is not a liability – yet. So the school fees you will have to pay over the next four years are not a liability at this moment, nor is the cost of maintaining your car next year.

Calculating your net worth

Take away total liabilities from total assets – the amount left is how much you are worth. This is called your *net worth*. For instance:

	£
at 30 June	
your assets are worth	16,000
you have liabilities of	4,000
your net worth is	12,000

Worked example

At midnight on 31 December 19XX, Graham Smith owned these assets, and had these liabilities:

- A house worth £100,000 on which £25,000 was still owing to a building society;
- A car worth £5,000 – Graham still owed £2,000 under a hire purchase agreement for the car;
- Furniture worth £8,500;
- Cash in a savings account £1,900;
- Graham owed £230 for things he bought with a credit card. He will pay this amount by the end of January.

On 31 December there was a serious leak in the roof of Graham's house. He has not yet had the roof repaired. But Graham must have the repair done very soon. You must *provide* for the probable cost of about £500. Include a *provision* of £500 as if it were already a liability at 31 December, because the roof was already faulty at that date.

Have a go at making a list of Graham Smith's assets and liabilities at 31 December 19XX in Figure 1.1, and work out his net worth.

Calculation of Graham Smith's net worth at 31 December 19XX

Liabilities	£	Assets	£
Owing to building society	25,000	House	100,000
Hire purchase on car	2,000	Car	5,000
Credit card	230	Furniture	8,500
Provision for roof repairs	500	Cash in savings account	1,900
	27,730		115,400

	£
Assets	115,400
Less: Liabilities	27,730
Net worth	87,670

Another name for Graham's net worth of £87,670 is his *capital*. Graham's capital is the amount that belongs to him. If he sold all his assets, and paid off all his liabilities, he would be left with his capital – £87,670.

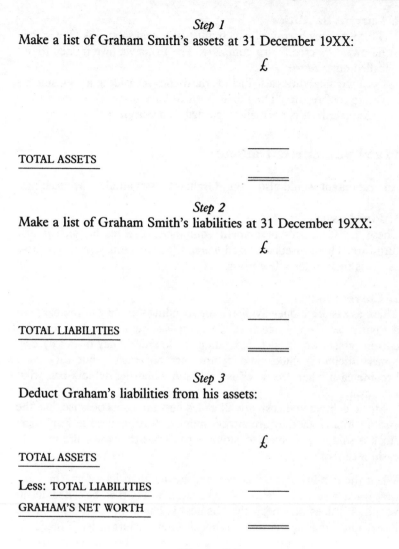

Step 1
Make a list of Graham Smith's assets at 31 December 19XX:

£

TOTAL ASSETS

Step 2
Make a list of Graham Smith's liabilities at 31 December 19XX:

£

TOTAL LIABILITIES

Step 3
Deduct Graham's liabilities from his assets:

£

TOTAL ASSETS

Less: TOTAL LIABILITIES

GRAHAM'S NET WORTH

Figure 1.1

Liabilities

An accountant would group Graham's liabilities under two headings:

1. Medium-/long-term liabilities
This is money borrowed and repayable in more than one year – the building society loan, the hire purchase loan.

2. Current liabilities

This is money borrowed which must be repaid soon – like the money he owes the credit card company. The firms we owe money to are called our *creditors*.

Current liabilities also include the money set aside as a provision for future roof repairs. The repair bill will have to be paid soon.

An overdraft is normally regarded as a current liability.

Fixed and current assets

An accountant would also group Graham's assets under two headings:

1. Fixed assets

These are Graham's permanent equipment, like his house, car and furniture. These assets are fixed *financially*. The money spent on these assets is tied up for a few years.

2. Current assets

These assets are money available for spending – money in the bank, in a savings account, in cash. If Graham was running a business, his current assets would include trading stock, and money owing by customers (debtors). Stock and debtors are not cash – but they soon become cash when the stock is sold, and when the debtors pay what they owe.

Stock, debtors and cash are all called current assets because, like the current in a river, they are always moving. Cash is used to buy stock, stock is sold to customers, customers pay what they owe, and we hold cash once more.

When the liabilities of a business are greater than its assets, the business has a *'negative net worth'*. The business would then be called 'insolvent'. This does not mean the business is bankrupt or in liquidation. Bankruptcy and liquidation only result after a court order is made.

Officially, a current asset is an asset which will turn into cash within a year of the balance sheet date.

Here is another way of setting out Graham's liabilities and assets in which we make both liabilities and assets add up to the same total.

We do this by including Graham's capital at the top of the liabilities list. This works because the amount of capital is the difference between the total of the assets and the liabilities.

The balance sheet

Both sides now 'balance'. We can call this a *balance sheet* (see Figure 1.2).

Graham Smith

Balance sheet as at 31 December 19XX

Liabilities		Assets	
(SOURCES OF FINANCE)		(APPLICATION OF FINANCE)	
CAPITAL	£	FIXED ASSETS	£
Graham Smith	87,670	House	100,000
MEDIUM-/LONG-TERM		Car	5,000
LIABILITIES		Furniture	8,500
		CURRENT ASSETS	
Building society	25,000	Cash in savings	
Hire purchase	2,000	account	1,900
CURRENT LIABILITIES			
Credit card	230		
Provision for			
roof repairs	500		
	115,400		115,400

Figure 1.2

A balance sheet is always at a point in time. This balance sheet is as at midnight on 31 December 19XX.

Sources and uses of finance

Sources of finance
The liabilities side of Graham's balance sheet is also headed *Sources of Finance*. Graham's assets are financed from three sources:

1. His own money – his capital. Why do we call capital a 'liability'? Because accountants see a balance sheet as quite separate from its owner. So the capital is seen as money owing to the owner. Remember this point – it is important.

   We can think of capital as an 'internal' liability. (Capital is a difficult

7

word. We use it to mean several different things. In this book you will learn about capital *expenditure* – money spent on machinery, buildings, etc. You will learn about *working* capital – the cushion of money a business uses to trade with. But when we talk about *Graham Smith's capital* we mean the money that belongs to him.)

2. Medium-/long-term liabilities } Money borrowed from outsiders –
3. Current liabilities } banks, creditors, etc.

Application of finance
The assets side shows what Graham was doing with his capital and borrowings at the stroke of midnight on 31 December 19XX. The money was in the form of fixed and current assets.

Self-check

Do all the self-check questions we set. They won't take long, but they will strengthen your knowledge and pick up any misunderstandings.

For each of the following questions, we give four possible answers. Put a ring around the letter (a, b, c or d) you think is correct. Then check against the answers at the end of the self-check. Where you get an answer wrong, look back through the chapter to see what you missed or misunderstood.

1. Which one of these is an asset?
   (a) Loan from building society (b) Capital (c) Stock (d) Provision for repainting
2. Which one of these is a liability?
   (a) Debtors (b) Cash (c) Wages owing (d) Buildings
3. At 30 June Arnold Green has the following assets and liabilities. How much was his net worth?
   Machinery £20,000; debtors £8,000; overdraft £3,000; creditors £5,000.
   (a) £20,000 (b) £10,000 (c) £14,000 (d) £4,000
4. Arnold Green's capital at 30 June was:
   (a) £4,000 (b) £26,000 (c) £14,000 (d) £20,000
5. Speedy Transport Ltd runs a bus service. Which one of the following assets of the firm is a fixed asset?
   (a) Stock of petrol (b) Cash at bank (c) Buses (d) Debtors
6. With Speedy Transport Ltd, which one of these is a current asset?
   (a) Stock of petrol (b) Buses (c) Buildings (d) Office furniture

7. Which one of these is a current liability?
   (a) Three-year loan from the bank (b) Wages owing (c) Mortgage loan
   (d) Capital
8. Which one of these is a medium-/long-term liability?
   (a) Accrued wages (ie wages owing) (b) Three-year loan from the bank
   (c) Provision for repainting (d) Capital
9. Which one of these is true?
   (a) Capital is money spent on assets like machinery;
   (b) Capital is money owing to the owner;
   (c) Capital is current assets less current liabilities;
   (d) Capital is the excess of liabilities over assets.

Answers
1c, 2c, 3a, 4d, 5c, 6a, 7b, 8b, 9b.

Chapter 2
The Narrative Style

Narrative style balance sheets

There are many ways of setting out balance sheets. In Chapter 1 we set out Graham's balance sheet in the 'old fashioned' style. Figure 2.1 shows his balance sheet in the *narrative style* – it tells clearly the story of Graham's finances.

The top part of the balance sheet shows *capital employed*. Capital employed means Graham's capital *plus* medium-/long-term liabilities.

The capital employed in Graham's life is £114,670. What was he doing with his money at the stroke of midnight on 31 December 19XX?

The answer is in the second part of the balance sheet – headed *Employment of Capital*:

- £113,500 was tied up in fixed assets
- £1,170 was being used as working capital

The amount of working capital is calculated by taking away the total current liabilities from the total current assets (because the current liabilities will be paid off from the current assets).

Working capital is the cushion of money Graham keeps so that he can pay what he owes – on time. Graham has only a small amount of working capital, but it is enough for his needs. If he were running a business he would need much more working capital. Not only to pay wages and creditors on time, but so that he could buy sufficient trading stock, and also allow his customers time to pay what they owe.

Graham Smith
Balance Sheet as at 31 December 19XX

	£	£	£
CAPITAL			87,670
LONG-TERM LIABILITIES			
Building society		25,000	
Hire purchase		2,000	27,000
CAPITAL EMPLOYED			114,670

EMPLOYMENT OF CAPITAL

	£	£	£
FIXED ASSETS			
House	100,000		
Car	5,000		
Furniture	8,500		113,500
CURRENT ASSETS			
Savings account		1,900	
less: CURRENT LIABILITIES			
Credit card	230		
Provision for roof repairs	500	730	
NET CURRENT ASSETS			1,170
			114,670

Figure 2.1

Note: The total on page 7 – £115,400 – now becomes £114,670 because the current liabilities of £730 are now *deducted* from the assets.

Worked example

The capital of a business is the difference between the business's assets and its liabilities. Mr Phillips' business is called Townend Grocery. On 31 March 19XX the assets and liabilities of Townend Grocery were: Equipment £9,000; trading stock £12,000; debtors £3,200 (but make a provision for the possibility that 10 per cent of the debtors *may* not pay what they owe); cash at bank £1,200; creditors £4,100; wages owing £400; loan owing to RT Finance Ltd, payable over three years, £5,600.

Work out the capital of Townend Grocery on Figure 2.2. Then fill in the capital, assets and liabilities in Figure 2.3.

Calculation of Capital – Townend Grocery

Assets		Liabilities and provisions	
	£		£
TOTAL ASSETS	————	TOTAL LIABILITIES and PROVISIONS	————
	════		════

	£
TOTAL ASSETS	
Less: LIABILITIES and PROVISIONS	
	————
Gives: CAPITAL	════

Figure 2.2

**Mr Phillips trading as Townend Grocery
Balance Sheet as at 31 March 19XX**

£

CAPITAL (EQUITY) . . . .

MEDIUM-/LONG-TERM LIABILITIES ⎯⎯⎯

CAPITAL EMPLOYED

═══

EMPLOYMENT OF CAPITAL

FIXED ASSETS . . . .

CURRENT ASSETS

Stock	⎯⎯⎯
Debtors	⎯⎯⎯
Cash at bank	⎯⎯⎯
Total Current Assets	

═══

Less: CURRENT LIABILITIES

Creditors	⎯⎯⎯
Wages accrued	⎯⎯⎯
Provision for doubtful debts	⎯⎯⎯
Total Current Liabilities	

═══

NET CURRENT ASSETS

(Working Capital) . . . .

⎯⎯⎯

═══

Figure 2.3

Figure 2.4 shows what the finished result should be.

Mr Phillips trading as Townend Grocery
Balance Sheet as at 31 March 19XX

	£	£
CAPITAL (EQUITY)		14,980
MEDIUM-/LONG-TERM LIABILITIES		
RT Finance Ltd		5,600
CAPITAL EMPLOYED		20,580

EMPLOYMENT OF CAPITAL

FIXED ASSETS		9,000
Current Assets		
Stock	12,000	
Debtors	3,200	
Cash at bank	1,200	
Total Current Assets	16,400	
Less: CURRENT LIABILITIES		
Creditors	4,100	
Wages accrued	400	
Provision for doubtful debts	320	
Total Current Liabilities	4,820	
NET CURRENT ASSETS		11,580
(WORKING CAPITAL)		20,580

Figure 2.4

Some thoughts about Townend Grocery's balance sheet:

- We have called the capital *equity*. Equity is another word for capital – it is the amount belonging to the owner. If you own a house worth £50,000, and owe the building society £20,000, we would say that your equity in the house is £30,000. It is the bit that belongs to you.
- Mr Phillips' equity in his business is £14,980. This amount is 72.8 per

cent of the total capital employed of £20,580. This percentage will please the bank manager. Banks and other lenders, as a general rule, like at least 60 per cent of capital employed to be supplied by the owner of a business, and not more than 40 per cent to be borrowed as medium-/long-term loans. The problem with loans is that they have to be repaid from profits, or from fresh loans. Also, interest is usually payable on loans and this reduces the profits.

- The current assets total £16,400, the current liabilities £4,820.

The current assets are 3.4 times greater than the current liabilities:

$$\frac{16,400}{4,820} = 3.4$$

We say that the current ratio is 3.4 to 1. Ratios are like a football score, in which the away team always scores 1 goal. The score for Townend Grocery is Current Assets, 3.4; Current Liabilities, 1.

A current ratio of 2:1 or better suggests (but does not prove) that there is enough working capital. Enough working capital helps the business to operate smoothly – to hold sufficient stock and debtors, and to pay the wages and current liabilities on time.

Townend Grocery appears to have enough working capital.

Mr Phillips' personal financial position

Because equity is more than 60 per cent of capital employed, and the current ratio is more than 2:1, the balance sheet looks strong. But be warned: Townend Grocery is not a separate *legal* person from Mr Phillips – it is not a limited company. If the court were to declare Mr Phillips bankrupt because he cannot pay his personal debts, then Townend Grocery would be taken over by his trustee in bankruptcy together with all Mr Phillips' other assets. If you are thinking of lending money to Townend Grocery, be sure to check on Mr Phillips' *personal* financial position.

The strength of the balance sheet

You have made up this balance sheet from the amounts Mr Phillips gave us. Supposing he had given us the wrong amount for the stock? Instead of £12,000 the stock should have been £5,000. Would this make any difference to the equity? Would it make any difference to the 'strength' of the balance sheet? Yes, of course it would. The amounts of the equity and the current assets would both be reduced by £7,000. The percentage of equity, and the current ratio would both be reduced, and the balance sheet would look a lot weaker.

The appearance of a balance sheet depends on the values given for assets, liabilities and provisions. This is important.

Balance sheets relate to a point in time
A final thought: balance sheets show the assets and liabilities at a point in time. With Townend Grocery that time is midnight on 31 March 19XX. A balance sheet is like a photograph. A photograph of a wood at noon on 30 June will look very different from a photograph of the same wood on 31 December. The same applies with balance sheets. The balance sheet of Townend Grocery on 15 April 19XX might look very different indeed from that at 31 March 19XX. More money may have been borrowed, the amount of stock and debtors may have doubled, the amount of creditors fallen.

Self-check

1. AB Ltd has equity totalling £45,000, a loan from the bank repayable over three years of £15,000, an overdraft of £10,000 and creditors of £12,000. The capital employed in the company is:
   (a) £50,000 (b) £60,000 (c) £38,000 (d) £52,000
2. Working capital is:
   (a) Fixed assets (b) Fixed assets plus current assets (c) Equity plus loans (d) Current assets less current liabilities
3. At 31 March, DC Ltd had the following balances in its books: stock £30,000; creditors £20,000; debtors £25,000; machinery £50,000; wages accrued £8,000; cash at bank £4,000. The working capital of the company was:
   (a)£31,000 (b) £81,000 (c) £39,000 (d) 27,000
4. In TH Ltd current assets total £45,000 and current liabilities £15,000. The current ratio is therefore:
   (a) 3:1 (b) 1:3 (c) 4:1 (d) 1:4
5. The bank manager likes to see a current ratio of 2:1 or better because it suggests that:
   (a) There is enough capital invested in the business; (b) The business has sufficient fixed assets to operate with; (c) The business has enough working capital to operate with (d) The business can pay all its debts immediately.
6. Which of the following is a sign that a firm possibly does not have enough working capital?
   (a) Low profit; (b) Not enough equipment; (c) Low productivity; (d) Difficulty in paying creditors on due date.

7. The bank manager likes to see that a business's equity is greater than medium-/long-term borrowings because:
   (a) This means the firm will have enough working capital; (b) Medium-/long-term loans usually have to be repaid, equity is permanent finance; (c) The firm will then have sufficient fixed assets to operate with; (d) Not correct – the bank manager prefers to see *more* loans and *less* equity.
8. A limitation of balance sheets is that they:
   (a) Sometimes do not balance; (b) The directors can show any figures they like; (c) They are often produced too long after the financial year-end; (d) They only show the equity, assets and liabilities at one point in time.
9. In a balance sheet the stock is shown as £20,000. The true value of the stock is £12,000. As a result of this error:
   (a) Fixed assets and equity are overstated; (b) Fixed assets and equity are understated; (c) Working capital and equity are overstated; (d) Working capital and equity are understated.

Worked example
Try working out the equity for Excelsior Boots Ltd at 31 March 19XX, and then prepare a balance sheet, using the form in Figure 2.5. Figure 2.6 shows how the completed balance sheet should look.

Creditors £15,200; buildings £34,000; furniture £4,000; stock £20,500; 10-year loan from XY Finance Ltd £25,000; overdraft £5,700; debtors £17,300; machinery £20,000; cash £500; provision for leave pay £5,000; provision for bad debts £1,000.

CAPITAL (EQUITY) . . . .

MEDIUM-/LONG-TERM LIABILITIES _____

CAPITAL EMPLOYED _____

EMPLOYMENT OF CAPITAL

FIXED ASSETS

£

_____

_____

_____

Total Fixed Assets . . . .

CURRENT ASSETS

Stock _____
Debtors _____
Cash _____
Total Current Assets

_____

CURRENT LIABILITIES

Creditors _____
Overdraft _____
Provisions: Bad debts _____
         Leave pay _____

Total Current Liabilities

_____

NET CURRENT ASSETS . . . .

(WORKING CAPITAL)

_____

_____

Figure 2.5

Excelsior Boots Ltd
Balance Sheet as at 31 March 19XX

	£
CAPITAL (EQUITY)	44,400
MEDIUM-/LONG-TERM LIABILITIES	25,000
CAPITAL EMPLOYED	69,400

EMPLOYMENT OF CAPITAL

FIXED ASSETS

Buildings	34,000	
Furniture	4,000	
Machinery	20,000	
Total Fixed Assets		58,000

CURRENT ASSETS

Stock	20,500	
Debtors	17,300	
Cash	500	
Total Current Assets	38,300	

CURRENT LIABILITIES

Creditors	15,200	
Overdraft	5,700	
Provisions: Bad debts	1,000	
Leave pay	5,000	
Total Current Liabilities	26,900	

NET CURRENT ASSETS		11,400
(WORKING CAPITAL)		69,400

Figure 2.6

19

Chapter 3
Depreciation

The effect of profit on capital

Profit increases capital.

Suppose your capital is £10,000, and all the money is in the bank. You take the money and use it to buy a car costing £10,000.

You then sell the car for £11,000, and bank the money. Your capital has now increased from £10,000 to £11,000. The amount of the increase, £1,000, is the profit you made on buying and selling the car. Profit therefore increases capital.

Figure 3.1 shows how your balance sheet would look:

Before the car deal	£	*After* the car deal	£
Capital	10,000	Capital	10,000
		Add: profit	1,000
		New capital	11,000
Employment of capital		Employment of capital	
Bank	10,000	Bank	11,000

Figure 3.1

If you made a loss on the sale of the car, your capital would have been reduced.

Replacing equipment

XY Earthmovers Ltd made a profit of £50,000 in the year ended 31 March 1999.

Figure 3.2 shows the company's balance sheet at that date. (We use the 'old fashioned' style because it makes our demonstration easier to follow.)

XY Earthmovers Ltd
Balance Sheet as at 31 March 1999

Liabilities		Assets	
(Sources of finance)		(Application of finance)	
	£		£
Equity	250,000	Equipment	150,000
Add: profit for the year	50,000	Working capital	210,000
New equity	300,000		
Loan from RX Ltd	60,000		
	360,000		360,000

Figure 3.2

The owner of the company, Charles Ogden, decides that he would like to pay the profit of £50,000 to himself, as a dividend on his equity of £250,000. His accountant has a different idea.

'Mr Ogden, what about replacing the equipment?'

'What do you mean?' responds Charles.

'Well, that equipment of yours – bulldozers, rollers and so on, won't last forever. You will have to replace it one day. How long will the equipment last?'

'I should say about five years,' replies Charles.

'Then don't you think it would be a good idea to set aside some of the profit each year over the next five years? Then you will have the money to replace the equipment in five years' time.'

Provision for depreciation

Charles agrees. They decide to set aside from the profits, every year for the next five years, one fifth of the cost of the equipment. The amount set aside each year will be £150,000 divided by 5 – £30,000.

The amount of profit set aside is called a *provision for depreciation*.

Figure 3.3 shows the balance sheet *after* making the provision for depreciation.

Note. Depreciation is usually thought of as writing off the cost of assets against profits. But there is more to it than that. We are concerned with the effects of depreciation on the finances of a business. So we emphasise provision for depreciation as a process of holding back profits to finance replacement.

XY Earthmovers Ltd
Balance Sheet as at 31 March 1999

Liabilities			Assets	
(Sources of finance)			(Application of finance)	
	£	£		£
Equity		250,000	Equipment	150,000
Add: profit	50,000		Working capital	210,000
for the year				
Less:				
Depreciation	13,000	20,000		
New equity		270,000		
Provision for				
depreciation		30,000		
Loan from RX Ltd		60,000		
		360,000		360,000

Figure 3.3

Mr Ogden can now only pay himself a dividend of £20,000. The provision for depreciation, £30,000, stays behind in the company.

The provision will be increased by £30,000 every year, and in five years' time, the provision for depreciation will total £150,000.

Q. *You say that £30,000 will be set aside each year. Where will this money be? In the bank?*

A. Well, the £30,000 is part of the year's profit and when we make a profit, it increases the money in the bank. But few businesses leave money sitting in the bank. They use it for expansion, for buying more stocks, increasing the equipment, and so on. By 31 March 2003, the money which represents the provision of £150,000 may have been used to buy extra bulldozers, or it may be in the form of stocks, or debtors, as well as in the bank.

Q. *But if the £150,000 is not in the bank, how will XY Earthmovers find the cash to replace the equipment?*

A. Quite a problem. However, even if the £150,000 is not in the bank, the company will be financially stronger because of the money invested in other assets. The company should therefore be able to borrow money for the replacement. In any case, what usually happens is that replacement does not take place all at once. Replacement takes place over a number of years. So the profit held back as depreciation in a year is often similar in amount to the money spent on replacing equipment in the same year.

Sinking fund

A good idea would be to take £30,000 each year out of the bank account and invest it in a deposit account. Then, by 31 March 2003 there would be £150,000 in a deposit account available for replacing the equipment. We call the deposit account (or other form of investment) a *sinking fund*. But few companies will put the depreciation provision into a sinking fund. They would rather leave the money in the business. They can then use the money to buy extra equipment, or stocks, or open a new branch. The companies will reckon they can make far more profit by investing the money in this way – compared with the interest they would earn in a deposit account.

Inflation

Is there serious price inflation in your country? If so you will be thinking that the cost of replacing XY Earthmover's equipment, in five years, will be much greater than the historical cost of the equipment. £150,000 will not be enough to pay for the replacement of the equipment. Some companies cope with the effect of inflation by increasing the balance sheet value of their fixed assets to replacement values. The yearly depreciation is then worked out on this replacement value. This means that the annual depreciation charge is automatically increased to cover the increased cost of replacement. We explain how the revaluation of assets is done on pages 29–31.

In Britain and other countries, a system called 'current cost accounting' (CCA for short) has been recommended. Appendix B is a brief description of the system. Few companies use it. If, as is usual, a company does not use CCA, the company may, however, publish a *supplementary* balance sheet, additional to the normal 'historical' balance sheet, showing how the balance sheet would appear *if* CCA were used. The CCA balance sheet *usually* shows smaller profits than the historical balance sheet – but not always. It took the accounting bodies in Britain many years to decide on the CCA system, but the system is still a bone of contention.

Book value

In the balance sheet, the provision for depreciation is usually deducted from the cost of the fixed asset, as shown overleaf.

Equipment

Cost	Less: provision for depreciation	Book value
£150,000	£30,000	£120,000

Each year the provision gets bigger, and the book value smaller. With XY Earthmovers, by 31 March 2003, the equipment will appear in the balance sheet like this:

Cost	Less: provision for depreciation	Book value
£150,000	£150,000	nil

No more depreciation will be set aside from the profits because the equipment has now been 'written off'. Until the equipment is sold or scrapped, it will appear in the balance sheet at a nil value.

Book value is simply a mathematical calculation – cost less accumulated depreciation. Book value is not *true* value. Anyway, how much is 'true value'? If Charles Ogden sold XY Earthmovers as a going concern, he would get a good price for the equipment. But if he had to sell the equipment piecemeal at an auction sale, he would get far less. The auction sale price is called *break-up value*. But balance sheets are nearly always prepared supposing that the business is a *going concern*.

Although the book value is just a calculated figure, accountants try to make sure that there is not too great a gulf between the book value and the going concern value of the assets. They arrange this by using a depreciation rate and method which is right for each kind of asset. In Appendix A we give some information about depreciation methods.

Q. *Supposing we do not intend to replace the asset. Do we still depreciate it if the asset is losing value, or is wearing out?*

A. The International Accounting Standards (recommendations of the International Accounting Standards Committee set up in 1973) say we must.

(The accounting bodies in each member country undertake to support the International Standards and try to ensure that published accounts in their country comply with the standards. In the United Kingdom this is done through the issue of Statements of Standard Accounting Practice – SSAP.)

Q. *But what happens to the profit we then set aside if it is not used for replacement?*

A. Well, the money just remains in the business – in the form of current and, perhaps, new fixed assets. What has happened is that the old asset, as it is written down by depreciation, is gradually being changed into cash and new assets – at the expense of profit. This process is called *maintaining the capital base*.

Self-check

True or False?
Try answering these questions. Put a circle around T if you think a statement is true – and a circle round F if you think it is false.
Important – you may refer to the chapter as often as you like – but once you have made a circle, you are not allowed to change it! Check your score at the end.

1. If you sell something and make a profit you increase your assets.   T F
2. If you sell something at a profit you increase your capital.   T F
3. The only way to increase the capital of your business is to make a profit.   T F
4. We can provide for the cost of replacing fixed assets by setting aside profit in a provision for depreciation.   T F
5. You can increase the capital of your business by borrowing money from the bank.   T F
6. By setting aside profit in a depreciation provision, you will have sufficient cash to pay for the replacement of the asset.   T F
7. The book value of an asset is calculated by deducting the year's depreciation from the cost of the asset.   T F
8. A provision for depreciation will not usually be represented by an equal amount of cash in the bank.   T F
9. Book value is always more or less equal to the realisation value of an asset.   T F
10. The International Accounting Standards say that all fixed assets must be depreciated.   T F
11. When the time comes to replace an asset, the amount of the provision will equal the cost of replacement.   T F
12. The book value of an asset is calculated by deducting the accumulated depreciation from the cost of the asset.   T F
13. A sinking fund is made up of cash, equal to the depreciation provision, specially invested.   T F

Answers
1T, 2T, 3F, 4T, 5F, 6F, 7F, 8T, 9F, 10F, 11F, 12T, 13T, 14T, 15T, 16T, 17T.

14. Because of inflation, the provision for depreciation is often less than the amount required to replace the asset. T F
15. The International Accounting Standards say that all fixed assets should be depreciated if they are losing value or wearing out. T F
16. Until it is used to replace the asset, the depreciation provision is a source of finance. T F
17. You can increase the capital of your business by making a profit, or by investing more money in the business. T F

Worked example

A *trial balance* is a list of the balances of the various accounts in a set of double entry books, at a point in time.

The *double entry* system of bookkeeping was developed in Italy in the thirteenth century. All well-run businesses use this system whether their books are handwritten, done on a machine or kept on a computer.

From the figures in the trial balance, the accountant prepares the balance sheet. Figure 3.4 shows the trial balance for Belinda Ceramics. From it, try preparing a balance sheet using the form in Figure 3.5. Then check your answer from Figure 3.6. You do not need to work out the equity for Belinda Ceramics – the equity is one of the accounts in the ledger.

Trial Balance at 31 March 19XX

	£	£
Equity		31,500
Long-term loan		15,000
Land (cost)	15,000	
Vehicles (cost)	22,000	
Provision for depreciation of vehicles		3,000
Stock	6,000	
Debtors	8,000	
Cash at bank	3,000	
Creditors		3,000
Provision for bad debts		1,000
Provision for leave pay		500
	54,000	54,000

Figure 3.4

Belinda Ceramics Ltd
Balance Sheet as at 31 March 1999

£

CAPITAL (EQUITY)
MEDIUM-/LONG-TERM BORROWINGS

CAPITAL EMPLOYED

EMPLOYMENT OF CAPITAL

FIXED ASSETS

	Cost	*Provision for depreciation*	*Book value*
Land			
Vehicles			
Total			

CURRENT ASSETS

Stock	
Debtors	
Cash at bank	
Total Current Assets	

Less: CURRENT LIABILITIES

Creditors	
Provisions:	
Bad debts	
Leave pay	
Total Current Liabilities	

NET CURRENT ASSETS

(WORKING CAPITAL)

Figure 3.5

Belinda Ceramics Ltd
Balance Sheet as at 31 March 1999

	£
CAPITAL (EQUITY)	31,500
MEDIUM-/LONG-TERM BORROWINGS	15,000
CAPITAL EMPLOYED	46,500

EMPLOYMENT OF CAPITAL

FIXED ASSETS

	Cost	Provision for depreciation	Book value	
Land	15,000		15,000	
Vehicles	22,000	3,000	19,000	
Total	37,000	3,000	34,000	34,000

CURRENT ASSETS

Stock	6,000
Debtors	8,000
Cash at bank	3,000
Total Current Assets	17,000

Less: CURRENT LIABILITIES

Creditors	3,000
Provisions:	
Bad debts	1,000
Leave pay	500
Total Current Liabilities	4,500

NET CURRENT ASSETS	12,500
(WORKING CAPITAL)	46,500

Figure 3.6

28

Chapter 4
Fixed Assets

Capital and revenue expenditure

Fixed assets are shown in the balance sheet at cost less depreciation provision.

The cost of a fixed asset includes what was paid for the asset, plus the cost of installation, and the cost of any improvement. The cost of repairs and maintenance of a fixed asset is not shown in the balance sheet, but is deducted from profits. This is because repairs and maintenance add nothing to the original value of the assset – they simply restore the asset to its original condition.

Money spent on acquiring fixed assets is called *capital expenditure*.

Money spent on maintenance, as well as all other expenditure deducted from profits, like wages, rent, interest, etc, is called *revenue expenditure*.

Revaluation

The International Accounting Standards say that all assets which wear out should be depreciated.

Buildings wear out, or become obsolete or old fashioned. But because of inflation or because the building is in a good trading position, the value of a building often *increases*. This increase in value is called *appreciation*.

Figure 4.1 shows the balance sheet of OJ Properties Ltd at 30 June 19XX:

	£
Share capital	600,000
Employment of capital	
Land and buildings (at cost)	600,000

Figure 4.1

At 30 June 19XX, the directors decide to increase the value of the land and buildings to their present market value. They ask for a report from a firm of valuers, who report that the land and buildings now have an open market value of £900,000. The accountant is asked to make an adjustment in the books; Figure 4.2 shows the balance sheet at 30 June 19XX:

OJ Properties Ltd
Balance Sheet as at 30 June 19XX

	£
Share capital	600,000
Capital reserve	
Increase in value of land and buildings	300,000
Equity	900,000
Employment of capital	
Land and buildings (as valued)	900,000

Figure 4.2

The company has made a *paper profit* of £300,000. Paper profits are included under a heading *Capital reserve*. The expression capital reserve comes from the Companies Act. The paper profit of £300,000 cannot be paid out as a dividend ('distributed') because the profit is not represented by cash in the bank. We therefore say a capital reserve is *non-distributable*.

The paper profit included in capital reserve, however, belongs to the shareholders. Therefore it is included as part of their equity.

In the United Kingdom the reserve would be called a 'revaluation reserve'.

If the buildings are being depreciated, the increase in their value will mean that the annual depreciation – deducted from profits – will also increase.

Bonus shares

The shareholders of OJ Properties agree to convert the capital reserve into shares – 300,000 shares with a face value of £1 each. These shares would then be issued to the shareholders free of charge – one free (bonus) share for every two shares already held. After issuing the bonus shares, the balance sheet would then read as shown in Figure 4.3.

Capital employed	£
Share capital	900,000

Employment of capital	
Land and buildings (as valued)	900,000

Figure 4.3

Note that:
- The shareholders will then hold the shares with a face value more or less equal to the value of the assets of the company. This can be important if the shares are not quoted on a Stock Exchange, because if there is no quoted market price, the average shareholder will have little idea of the true value of his or her share holding.*
- If the shares *are* quoted on a Stock Exchange, a sudden increase in the number of shares in issue will result in the quoted share price falling proportionately. However, in practice this fall in the quoted price is often less than proportionate, and the shareholders gain from the issue.
- If the bonus issue is moderate in proportion to the existing share capital, the company will often maintain the dividend per share at the rate applying before the issue. This will maintain the quoted price of each share at its pre bonus-issue level, and the total market value of each shareholder's investment will therefore increase as a result of the issue.

Revaluation changes equity
Revaluing land and buildings (and sometimes other fixed assets) makes a big difference to a balance sheet. It changes the assets, and also the amount of equity. (The equity of OJ Properties was increased by £300,000). Balance sheet analysts make important calculations based on the amount of equity. But different companies have different policies about revaluing. These different policies can make it very difficult to compare the balance sheet of one company with that of another. This is an important point to remember.

---

* Many years ago, the BBC broadcast a play about the affairs of a family-owned woollen manufacturing company in Yorkshire. Part of the plot concerned a financier who bought control of the company by sending out agents to visit family members who held shares in the company. For instance, old Aunt Mary had a share certificate for 100 shares of £1 each. The agent offered her £300 for the certificate. Aunt Mary happily sold her shares. In fact, the assets behind Aunt Mary's shares were worth £2,000 because the company's woollen mill, in the middle of Leeds, as a development site, was worth 20 times the value shown in the balance sheet. But the directors had never revalued the mill and distributed bonus shares. Had the directors revalued the mill and issued bonus shares, then Aunt Mary would have been holding share certificates totalling £2,000.

Final thought

TDA Ltd revalues its assets and increases its equity. The amount of annual earnings is much the same after the revaluation as before. But, because the equity is now greater, the *percentage* of earnings to equity is smaller after the revaluation than before. Does this lower percentage show the true earnings story? How will this fall in percentage affect the thinking of someone about to buy shares in TDA Ltd?

Leased assets

XY Earthmovers Ltd need a new bulldozer but cannot afford to pay cash. The company can use one of two ways to pay for the bulldozer.

(a) **Hire purchase**

The company would pay a deposit to the seller, and pay off the balance by instalments over the next five years.

(b) Lease

The company would rent the bulldozer from the seller and pay a monthly rental over the next five years. At the end of the five years, XY Earthmovers can buy the bulldozer for a final payment of, say, £500. The rental that XY Earthmovers would pay each month over five years is enough to pay for the bulldozer, plus interest. This lease agreement is just another way of paying for the bulldozer.

Once signed, such a lease agreement cannot be cancelled by XY Earthmovers. This sort of lease is called a *finance lease*. (The sort of lease under which the lessee is simply using the asset, and will never own it, is called an *operating lease*.)

Hire purchase versus leasing

Charles Ogden will have to decide whether to use leasing or hire purchase. He will decide which method gives the best income tax advantage, or the easiest repayment rate, or the lowest interest charge.

If Charles decides to use hire purchase, the new bulldozer will appear in the company's balance sheet as a fixed asset. At the same time, the amount owing to the hire purchase company will appear as a medium-/long-term liability. But if he decides to use leasing, the bulldozer might not appear in the balance sheet, because it will not belong to XY Earthmovers. The bulldozer belongs to the leasing company – until the end of the five years.

But a basic rule in the International Accounting Standards is that, in preparing financial statements, financial transactions should be shown in accordance with their *substance*, and not merely in accordance with their legal *form*. In Britain and the United States, for instance, it is usual to show an asset leased under a finance lease as a fixed asset in the balance sheet, and show the remaining instalments (excluding the interest charge) as a liability. *Legally* the leased asset does not belong to the company. But the *substance* of the agreement is that the company is buying the asset by instalments.

Where the lease hire asset is *not* shown in the balance sheet, we call the leasing arrangement *off balance sheet financing*. Where the asset is not shown in the balance sheet, details of the lease should be shown as a note to the balance sheet. This note is important because it reveals 'assets' and 'liabilities' not shown in the balance sheet. If these off balance sheet assets and liabilities were added to the assets and liabilities shown in the balance sheet, the financial position of the company might look very different.

Lease back

A variation of leasing is called *lease back*. Lease back is very often used with buildings. For example, JK Properties needs cash for expansion, so the company sells its office block to PK Finance Ltd which then 'leases back' the office block to JK Properties. JK Properties pays a rental over the next 10 years. (This rental is sufficient to buy back the office block over 10 years.)

Self-check

1. LZ Ltd has a share capital of £70,000. The company has only one asset – a building costing £70,000. The directors have the building valued. Its value is now £120,000. They decide to show the new value in the balance sheet. Which of the balance sheets in Figure 4.4 shows the revaluation correctly?
2. Which one of the following is *not* a correct statement about a capital reserve?
   (a) A capital reserve can be converted into bonus shares.
   (b) A capital reserve can usually be paid out as a dividend.
   (c) A capital reserve includes the amount of paper profit resulting from revaluation of property.
   (d) A capital reserve is described as 'non-distributable'.
3. It is a good idea to revalue land and buildings periodically because:

(a) There are income tax advantages.
(b) Dividends can increase.
(c) The amount of equity is more truly shown.
(d) The annual depreciation charge is reduced.

4. GH Ltd acquires a lathe under an irrevocable lease agreement with YN Finance Ltd. GH decides to treat the monthly rental as a deduction from profits and will omit the lathe from the balance sheet. Which one of the following is *not* true about this arrangement?

(a) It is illegal for GH Ltd to omit the lathe from their balance sheet.

(b) The capital portion of the rental paid by GH Ltd is, in effect, an asset of GH Ltd, and the remaining instalments a liability.

(c) Until the end of the lease period, the lathe belongs to YN Finance Ltd.

(d) The arrangement is known as 'off balance sheet financing'.

(a)	£	(b)	£
Share capital	70,000	Share capital	120,000
Profit	50,000		
Equity	120,000	Equity	120,000
Building (as valued)	120,000	Building (as valued)	120,000

(c)		(d)	
Share capital	70,000	Share capital	70,000
Capital reserve	50,000	Revenue reserve	50,000
Equity	120,000	Equity	120,000
Building (as valued)	120,000	Building (as valued)	120,000

Figure 4.4

Chapter 5
Goodwill

An intangible asset

You buy a dress shop in the main shopping area of your town. You pay £90,000 for the business. These are the assets you take over:

	£
Fittings	10,000
Stock	43,000
	53,000

You are paying £37,000 more for the business than the 'tangible' assets are worth. Why? Because the business is in a good position, it has a good reputation, and a lot of customers. You are paying £37,000 for the *goodwill* of the business.

Figure 5.1 shows the balance sheet of the business after you bought it.

	£
Capital	90,000
Employment of capital	
Goodwill	37,000
Fixed assets	
Fittings	10,000
Current assets	
Stock	43,000
	90,000

Figure 5.1

Goodwill is called an *intangible asset* because it 'cannot be touched', or is not a legal claim like a book debt.

The goodwill appears as an asset. But many accountants favour removing the goodwill from the balance sheet because usually goodwill cannot be sold off as a separate asset – the entire business must be sold. Also, the value of goodwill changes all the time with the ups and downs in the affairs of the business.

Goodwill is removed from the balance sheet by deducting it from reserves (which form part of the equity) as shown in Figure 5.2.

	£	£
Equity	90,000	
Less: goodwill written off	37,000	53,000
Fixed assets		
Fittings		10,000
Current assets		
Stock		43,000
		53,000

Figure 5.2

The write-off of the goodwill can also be spread over its 'payback period'. In the case of AZ Ltd (see below), the payback period would be three years.

When a bank manager sees a balance sheet containing goodwill he will, mentally, deduct the goodwill from the equity.

Formulas for goodwill
There are various formulas for working out the value of the goodwill of a business. Here is a commonsense way of calculating the goodwill of AZ Ltd, a long-established private college. We estimate that if we were to set up a new college in 1995 – instead of buying AZ Ltd – it would take three years to achieve the level of profit enjoyed by AZ Ltd, as shown in Figure 5.3.

It would be worth paying a *maximum* of £25,000 goodwill (£90,000 less £65,000) to acquire AZ Ltd, and immediately enjoy annual profits of £30,000 a year.

But, in the end, the goodwill is how much a buyer is prepared to pay for the business, over and above the realistic value of the tangible assets.

Cost of control
An asset, *cost of control*, sometimes appears in the consolidated balance

Annual Profits

	Our new college	AZ Ltd
1995	10,000	30,000
1996	25,000	30,000
1997	30,000	30,000
TOTAL	65,000	90,000

Figure 5.3

sheet of a group of companies. This is the amount the group holding company has had to pay, when buying a new subsidiary company, over and above the net worth of the subsidiary. The extra amount the holding company paid might be goodwill. But it would also result from the *tangible* assets of the subsidiary being undervalued in the subsidiary's balance sheet. In the United Kingdom, however, tangible assets acquired in a takeover must be valued at a 'fair value'.

Other intangible assets

Lease premiums
If you paid £20,000 to the previous tenant to buy over his lease to a property, you would show in your balance sheet £20,000 as an intangible asset – *lease premium*. If the lease has 10 years to run, you should write off £2,000 a year against profits. At the end of 10 years, the lease premium will then have been written down to nil.

Patents
If you pay £10,000 to buy an invention for a new kind of mouse trap, you would show the £10,000 in the balance sheet as an intangible asset – *patent*. The patent would be written off against profits over the expected life of the patent. The life of the patent, as far as a manufacturer is concerned, is how many years it will be before a rival starts manufacturing a better mouse trap.

Deferred revenue expenditure
A soap manufacturing company produces a new brand of detergent. In the first year £12 million is spent on introducing the product to the market – heavy advertising, thousands of free samples are given away and so on. The directors decide that the cost of the campaign should be spread over three years. In the first year, £4 million is charged against profits,

and £8 million is carried forward as an asset in the balance sheet. In the second year, a further £4 million is charged against profits, and again in the third year.

The cost of the campaign is, of course, revenue expenditure – an expense. The £8 million carried forward in the balance sheet is therefore called *deferred revenue expenditure* because the process of charging it against profits is being deferred. In theory, the cost of the campaign is charged against the additional profits the campaign generates over the three-year period.

Deferred revenue expenditure may also include money spent on developing new products.

Self-check

1. Which one of the following is an intangible asset?
   (a) Stock (b) Investment in AB Ltd (c) New development costs
   (d) Capital reserve
2. Which of the following is a tangible asset?
   (a) Goodwill (b) Cost of control (c) Deferred advertising costs
   (d) Motor vehicles
3. It is usual to remove the cost of goodwill from a balance sheet because:
   (a) It is fictitious;
   (b) It cannot easily be converted into cash;
   (c) The amount paid for it can never be recovered;
   (d) Goodwill has no value.
4. The cost of control represents:
   (a) The cost of acquiring the equity of a subsidiary;
   (b) The cost of acquiring the assets of a subsidiary;
   (c) The cost of acquiring the net worth of a subsidiary;
   (d) The cost of acquiring a subsidiary, less the amount of the net worth of the subsidiary acquired.
5. The purpose of carrying forward revenue expenditure in the balance sheet is:
   (a) To make the balance sheet look strong;
   (b) To spread a heavy expense over the years of its usefulness;
   (c) To improve the equity figure;
   (d) To avoid showing a loss.

Answers
1c, 2d, 3b, 4d, 5b.

Chapter 6
Current Assets

Stock

Current assets are assets which will become cash or be used up within 12 months of the date of the balance sheet. The current assets include stocks of finished goods, partly manufactured goods called *work in progress*, raw materials, spare parts and so on. Stock (also called 'inventory') is valued at cost (or cost of production) or market value, whichever is the less. Market value is the amount a stock item could be sold for in the ordinary course of business, less any selling costs. Market value is also called *net realisable value*.

The way stock is valued has a direct effect on profit. For example, if the value of stock in the balance sheet is increased by £100, the profit for the year will be increased by £100.

For this reason, accountants pay a lot of attention to how stock is valued. Here are some methods used.

First in first out (FIFO)
This method assumes that the first items of stock bought are the first sold. Stock is therefore valued at the actual prices paid for the latest quantities received.

Last in first out (LIFO)
This apparently totally illogical method assumes that the firm sells the *last* consignment received *first*. Therefore, stock is valued at what the items cost when the firm first started trading, perhaps many years ago. Because of inflation this means that the stock is usually undervalued. As a result, profits are understated. Consequently, less income tax is paid. LIFO is permitted by the United States taxation authorities and is therefore widely used in the USA because it reduces income tax.

One argument in favour of LIFO is that by understating profits, cash is being held back in the business. This cash helps finance the increasing cost of holding stocks which results from unit prices steadily increasing due to inflation.

Average cost

If the same stock has been bought or manufactured during the year at varying costs, then the stock at the end of the year can be valued at the *average* cost for the year.

Stock depreciation

The values of stock items which are becoming worth less and less due to age or obsolescence (fashionwear, spare parts, etc) are often reduced each year. These reductions in stock value are agreed with the income tax authorities, because the reductions reduce the profit.

Whichever stock valuation method is used, the accounting rule of consistency is vital – do not keep changing the valuation method from one year to the next. If the valuation method is changed, comparison of profit, one year with the next, becomes difficult.

It is important to remember that the stock valuation method has an immediate bearing on profit and equity.

Work in progress

As mentioned, this is part manufactured stock, going through a factory. It is valued at the cost of production so far.

Work in progress may also be work completed by a construction firm, not yet invoiced out to the client. This form of work in progress can amount to a very large sum, and the way it is valued makes a big difference to the annual profits.

Debtors

Bad debts will already have been removed from the total of debtors. A provision may have been made for doubtful debts. Doubtful debts are not bad, but the debtors are slow in paying.

The amount shown in the books as owing by hire purchase debtors often includes the finance charges due for the entire hire purchase contract. As the finance charges for *future* years have not been 'earned' at the date of the balance sheet, a provision is made for these future, unearned charges. Some very conservative companies also make a provision for the profit element included in instalments not yet due.

Bills receivable

In some lines of business it is common for debtors to sign ('accept') a *bill of exchange* in respect of the amount they owe. A bill of exchange is like a post-dated cheque, and is payable by the debtor in three months, six months or whatever time span is agreed. The amount of the bill is then deducted from the debtors and shown separately as a *bill receivable*. Bills receivable are often sold to a bank or finance house before due date. This is called *discounting a bill*. The bill then disappears from the balance sheet, and becomes cash at bank.

There is sometimes a danger that the acceptor of the bill will fail to honour it when the bank or finance house present it to him, on due date, for payment. The company which discounted the bill will then be obliged to refund the amount of the bill to the bank. For this reason, a note is added to the balance sheet reporting a *contingent liability* in respect of bills receivable which have been discounted, but are not yet payable by the acceptor.

Prepayments

Some expenses are normally paid in advance (*prepaid*): insurance premiums, property taxes, and the like. The amount prepaid at the date of the balance sheet and not yet 'used up' is shown as a current asset. For example, if the balance sheet is at 30 June, and insurance has been paid up to 30 September next, three months of insurance premium is prepaid at 30 June and appears as a current asset. From a bookkeeping point of view, the three months premium is being carried forward to the new financial year starting July, where it becomes an expense.

Cash at bank, in hand, short-term deposits, loans and investments

Where money is temporarily invested in shares quoted on a stock exchange, the investment will be shown in the balance sheet as a current asset, at cost. But a note must be added stating the market value of the shares at the date of the balance sheet. *Long-term* investments will be shown with the fixed assets.

Going concern

Stock and debtors (and indeed all assets) are valued on the assumption that the business is a going concern. Only rarely will assets be valued in the balance sheet on a break-up basis. The break-up of a business is a disaster because when a business is closed, many debtors simply disappear, and stock sold by auction or in bulk will bring perhaps less than half its cost value. Bank managers and other lenders are, however, interested in the break-up values because to recover their loan, they may in the end have to force a business into liquidation.

Self-check

True or False?

1. Reduce stock values, and you reduce profits.   T F
2. The FIFO method will normally result in a lower stock value than LIFO.   T F
3. Stock and debtors are normally valued on the basis of break-up value.   T F
4. Providing for unearned finance charges will reduce the profits for the year.   T F
5. The LIFO method of stock valuation usually results in reducing the reported profits of a business.   T F
6. An amount paid in advance at balance sheet date is shown as an asset.   T F
7. Stock is valued on the assumption that the business will carry on trading.   T F
8. Until a discounted bill receivable is honoured by the acceptor, a contingent liability exists towards the bank or finance house.   T F

Answers

1T, 2F, 3F, 4T, 5T, 6T, 7T, 8T.

Chapter 7
Liabilities

Medium-/long-term liabilities

Medium-/long-term liabilities are liabilities repayable in more than one year from the balance sheet date. They include loans from banks and finance houses, mortgage loans, amounts owing under hire purchase contracts and so on.

Usually these liabilities include instalments payable *within* one year, and the remaining instalments payable *after* a year. For example, a loan from TG Finance Ltd of £36,000 is payable by 36 monthly instalments of £1,000. We split the liability into two parts:

	£
Current portion – 12 instalments	12,000
Medium-/long-term liability – 24 instalments	24,000
	36,000

The current portion of £12,000 appears in the balance sheet under current liabilities, described as current portion of long-term liability. The £24,000 payable in more than one year is included under medium-/long-term liabilities.

Notes to the balance sheet will state the repayment terms of the medium-/long-term liabilities. Normally the finance to meet the repayments has to be found by earning profits. We therefore check whether the business is retaining enough profit at least equal to the repayment commitment. See 'Debt repayment ratio' – page 82.

Interest on loans is charged against profits. Only interest accrued to the date of the balance sheet but not yet paid will appear, as a current liability, in the balance sheet.

Deferred taxation

Deferred taxation is a difficult subject. You do not need to understand it completely, but it is important for you to know that the way in which deferred taxation is treated can make a big difference to after-tax profits and equity.

Deferred taxation is, in effect, a medium-/long-term liability. It is not money borrowed, but is profit set aside to meet a possible tax commitment. It is a provision.

For example, a company has revalued land and buildings, adding the paper profit of £150,000 to capital reserve. But if the land and buildings were to be sold, taxation of, say, £50,000 would be incurred on the profit of £150,000. The conservative, prudent, accountant will therefore suggest transferring profit of £50,000 to deferred taxation to provide for the future tax commitment – should the land and buildings ever be sold.

Timing differences

Most countries allow the full cost of fixed assets, like machinery, vehicles, furniture, equipment and so on, to be deducted from the profits before tax is calculated.

Some countries allow this deduction to be made year by year in the form of the annual depreciation charge.

But others, very generously, allow the *full cost* of the fixed asset to be deducted from the profits in the year in which the fixed asset is brought into use. This deduction is made on the income tax return. Once this deduction (often called a *capital allowance*) is made then, of course, the future annual depreciation ceases to be a tax deductible expense.

For example, NM Ltd bought a machine costing £300,000 in 1999. The directors decide to depreciate it by £60,000 a year.

Under the income tax law in their country, the full cost of the machine can be claimed as a capital allowance in 1999. Tax is calculated at 50 per cent of taxable income. The company's trading profit (before depreciation) in 1999 was £100,000.

Figure 7.1 shows the company's income tax return.

	£
Net profit for 1999	40,000
Add back depreciation (not tax deductible)	60,000
Taxable profit	100,000
Less: capital allowance (new machine)	300,000
Tax loss (carried forward to next year)	200,000
Tax payable	Nil

Figure 7.1

There are two possible balance sheets for NM Ltd, at 31 December 1999 at Figure 7.2:

(a) Making *no* adjustment for *deferred tax*		(b) Making an adjustment for *deferred tax*		
	£			£
Share capital	200,000	Share capital		200,000
Add:		Add:		
Net profit	40,000	Net profit	40,000	
		Less: Deferred tax		
		50 per cent	20,000	20,000
Equity		Equity		220,000
(capital employed)	240,000			
		Long-term liability		
		Deferred taxation		20,000
		Capital employed		240,000
Employment of capital		Employment of capital		
Various assets	240,000	Various assets		240,000

Figure 7.2

With (a), no taxation will be deducted from the profits so long as the tax loss is being carried forward. But as soon as the tax loss is used up, and the company starts to pay tax again, the tax burden will be much greater than 50 per cent of the net profit because the annual depreciation expense of £60,000 is not tax deductible, and is added back on the tax return.

With (b), the net profit is reduced by the appropriate taxation for the year, even though payment of this tax is deferred until the assessed loss is used up. As a result equity is reduced, and long-term liabilities are increased.

(In Appendix C we compare the results of methods (a) and (b) over a five-year period.)

With (b) the tax burden is always the same – 50 per cent of profits. There are no violent ups and downs in the tax burden.

With most businesses, however, the deferred taxation is unlikely to 'crystallise' into an actual liability, because companies are buying new equipment every year and claiming capital allowances. Where this is so, the International Accounting Standards say that companies need only set aside profit for deferred taxation where the deferred taxation is *likely* to crystallise into an actual liability.

Setting aside profit as deferred taxation only where the taxation is likely to crystallise into an actual liability is called the 'partial allocation method'. The amount of deferred taxation over and above the amount set aside under the partial allocation method is then merely shown as a note to the balance sheet. (See our notes on Marks and Spencer's balance sheet, Appendix D, page 95.)

A thought

Setting aside from profits the *full* amount of deferred taxation means that an equal amount of money is held back in the business and not paid out as dividends. This will strengthen the finances of the business. One is impressed by a balance sheet with deferred taxation provided for in full. Also the percentage of tax deducted from the profits each year will be constant.

A company which does not provide in full for deferred tax is placing reliance on continued investment in fixed assets and continued capital allowances. But supposing investment slows down or stops, maybe due to recession? Or the government reduces the initial capital allowance percentage (as happened in Britain in 1985)? Then the company may experience a sharply increased tax bill, for which no provision was made in past years. The result could be sharply reduced after-tax earnings.

Gearing (or 'leverage')

High and low gearing
Here is the first part of the balance sheet of TT Ltd:

	£
Equity	40,000
Medium-/long-term loans	80,000
Capital employed	120,000

Equity (£40,000) is 33.33 per cent of capital employed (£120,000). Borrowings are high, equity is low. When borrowings are high and equity low, we say the company is *high geared*. Think of the borrowings as the power drive. The power drive of £80,000 is turning round the equity of £40,000. The equity spins round twice as fast as the borrowings – like your car when you are driving in high gear. With high gearing we are getting much more mileage out of the equity – making each pound of equity more productive. We are getting this result by using other people's money to power our business.

Of course, we have to pay interest on the borrowings, so we must be sure that the profit we are making on each pound of borrowed money is greater than the interest we pay. And don't forget, we have to repay the borrowings one day.

The trading profit of TT Ltd for the year was £23,000. From this we deduct interest on the loans (10 per cent per annum), £8,000. The net profit is therefore £15,000. This net profit is a return of 37.5 per cent on the owner's investment (equity) of £40,000. This is an excellent return on equity. Compare it with the best interest rate you can get in your country on a long-term deposit with a bank.

Let us change the figures. Suppose the balance sheet reads like this:

	£
Equity	80,000
Medium-/long-term loans	40,000
Capital employed	120,000

This is now a *low geared* business, because borrowings are low, equity high.

Suppose that the profit is still the same, £23,000. But this time – because the borrowings are reduced – the interest payment is £4,000 and the net profit is now £19,000, greater than before.

But the *return on equity* (£19,000 as a percentage of £80,000) – 23.7 per cent – is nearly a third *less* than 37.5 per cent.

Warning
High gearing can produce high returns on equity – but it can be risky. If profits fall, the interest burden can quickly result in a net loss. Also the borrowed money has to be repaid.

Good conditions for being highly geared are:

1. A steady line of business – no wild fluctuations in earnings.
2. Easily saleable assets – like good stocks, land and buildings, debtors, marketable investments. If the worst happens, the assets can be sold to pay off the loans.
3. Good financial management.

Investment companies, property companies, traders and the like are suitable for high gearing because these businesses normally enjoy a steady income and their assets are easily turned into cash. Manufacturing industries are less suitable, because machinery is often hard to sell.

The safety limit for the percentage of equity to capital employed differs with each kind of business. With property owning companies an equity percentage as low as 25 per cent would be acceptable (ie invest 25 per cent and borrow 75 per cent of the cost of a new building). With most businesses 60 per cent equity is usually thought to be the lower limit. But it all depends on the nature of the business, the prospects, and the skill of management.

How businesses become highly geared

Allan Murphy has a shoe shop in Sydney. He is very successful. The business is financed entirely from equity of $30,000. He decides to open a branch in Canberra. He borrows $40,000 to finance the branch. He has no difficulty in borrowing this money because most of the money will be invested in stock, and he has proved himself to be a good businessman, earning excellent profits in Sydney. Also, a shoe shop is a steady line of business. As soon as he borrows the $40,000, his business is highly geared, (equity $30,000, borrowings $40,000). If all goes well, he should greatly increase the return on his original equity.

High gearing with expenses

A business with a high proportion of fixed costs – like rent and equipment leasing payments – would also be called highly geared.

With a high proportion of fixed costs, a fall in income can quickly result in trading losses. A rise in income will result in a sharp increase in profits.

Current liabilities

Current liabilities are liabilities which must be paid off within one year of the balance sheet date. They include:

Creditors
Also called 'accounts payable'.

Accruals
These are liabilities which have built up to the date of the balance sheet, but are not actually payable at that date – like interest accrued up to 30 November, but not payable until the end of the quarter, 31 December

Bills payable
Where the company has accepted a bill to clear a liability to a trade creditor. (See 'Bills receivable' on page 41.)

Provisions
For income tax, dividends, leave pay, etc. The provision for doubtful debts is usually shown as a deduction from debtors.

Overdraft
Some overdrafts go on for years, but virtually all overdrafts are subject to recall by the bank at very short notice. Ideally, an overdraft should be self-adjusting and be represented by good current assets. For example, a toy manufacturer might arrange an overdraft during the middle months of the year when he is building up stock. The overdraft will automatically clear itself when the stock is sold in November/December. Overdrafts which are *not* represented by current assets, and are not self-adjusting, might best be converted into medium-term loans. It is not a good plan to finance long-term assets with short-term borrowing.

Self-check

1. A loan of £12,000 is repayable by monthly instalments over four years. The interest rate is 10 per cent per annum. When the loan first appears in the balance sheet, the current portion will be:
   (a) £12,000 (b) £3,000 (c) £1,200 (d) £300
2. Which one of the following is *not* an advantage of setting aside profit to provide in full for deferred taxation:
   (a) The annual percentage deduction for tax from profits is constant;
   (b) The maximum ultimate liability for tax is shown;
   (c) The finances of the company are strengthened;
   (d) The amount provided agrees with the income tax assessment.
3. The partial allocation method of providing for deferred tax:
   (a) Shows the maximum ultimate tax liability;
   (b) Shows the amount that will be due on the current tax assessment;
   (c) Shows the amount of deferred taxation which is likely to crystallise;
   (d) Shows the amount of tax payable within one year of the balance sheet date.

4. Which of the following is the most highly geared?
   (a) Equity   £50,000   Loans   £50,000
   (b) Equity   £20,000   Loans   £50,000
   (c) Equity   £30,000   Loans   £50,000
   (d) Equity   £50,000   Loans   £30,000
5. Which is *not* a desirable condition for high gearing?
   (a) Large cash balances;
   (b) A steady line of business;
   (c) Good, saleable, assets;
   (d) Good management.
6. The chief benefit of high gearing is:
   (a) Increased return on equity;
   (b) A stronger balance sheet;
   (c) More working capital;
   (d) Lower interest rate.
7. Which one of the following is *not* a current liability?
   (a) Accruals (b) Bills receivable (c) Overdraft (d) Creditors

Answers
1b, 2d, 3c, 4b, 5a, 6a, 7b.

Chapter 8
The Management of Working Capital

Working capital ratios

Figure 8.1 shows the working capital of DF Ltd.

	£
Stocks	20,000
Debtors	30,000
Bank	3,000
Total Current Assets	53,000
Less: Current Liabilities	
Creditors	25,000
Current portion, long-term loan	5,000
Total Current Liabilities	30,000
Working capital	23,000

Figure 8.1

Here are two important ratios.

Current ratio
To obtain this, divide DF Ltd's current assets by the current liabilities

$$\frac{53,000}{30,000} = 1.76$$

Express the ratio as 1.76:1 (current assets 1.76:current liabilities 1.0).

As the current ratio is less than 2:1, it is possible that the company may not have enough working capital.

Acid test (or liquidity) ratio

For this you divide cash plus debtors by current liabilities:

$$\frac{30,000 + 3,000}{30,000} = 1.1$$

Express the ratio as 1.1:1 (Cash plus debtors 1.1:Current liabilities 1).

The ratio should be 1:1 or better. The ratio for DF Ltd of 1.1:1 is slightly better than 1:1 and shows the company has more cash and 'near cash' (debtors) than it has current liabilities. DF Ltd should be able to pay its current liabilities on time.

But beware!
Do not jump to conclusions from ratios. They often mislead. For instance, if the debtors of £30,000 are only due to pay in six months' time, but the creditors of £25,000 must be paid within one month, then DF Ltd would have difficulties in paying its creditors on time despite having a good acid test ratio.

Shortage of working capital

Although a company is making good profits, it can still get into financial difficulties if it does not have enough working capital. Often one of the first signs of a shortage of working capital is that the company has difficulty in paying the weekly wages. As things get worse, there is difficulty in paying creditors. If payments to creditors are not made on due date, or only part of the money owing is paid and the rest carried forward, the company will get a bad credit character and it will become difficult to obtain credit terms. This worsens the liquidity situation.

Bones and blood
The fixed assets of a business are the bones and the muscle. The working capital of a business is its blood. If the blood is insufficient, or circulation is poor, then the business will develop anaemia, become weak and perhaps eventually perish.

The *quantity* of the working capital, and the *speed* of its circulation, are of great importance in the management of a business.

How much working capital?

William Lamb had always wanted to run his own printing business. He had saved up £20,000, so he resigned from his job as sales manager, and opened While U Wait Printshop on 1 June. William decided that if he bought all the printing equipment for cash, he would be able to pick up some machinery bargains. He spent £18,000 on machinery, leaving £2,000 in the bank as working capital. His balance sheet at 1 June reads as shown in Figure 8.2.

	£
Capital	20,000
Employment of capital	
Fixes assets	18,000
Working capital	2,000
	20,000

Figure 8.2

But William had to hold large stocks of paper and materials, and also some important customers expected 30-day terms. Because he had a limited amount of money in the bank, he bought the stocks of paper and material on credit.

Figure 8.3 shows the balance sheet after a month of operation.

Balance Sheet at 30 June

	£	£
Capital		20,000
Employment of capital		
Fixed assets		18,000
Current assets		
Stocks	9,000	
Debtors	1,000	
Bank	1,000	
Total Current Assets	11,000	
Less:		
Current liability		
Creditors	9,000	
Working capital		2,000
		20,000

Figure 8.3

Current ratio is 1.2:1 and acid test ratio 0.2:1. How will William pay his creditors, let alone pay the weekly wages?

With hindsight, William thought it would have been far wiser to leave about £9,000 as working capital, and buy some of the machinery on hire purchase. He would still have to meet the hire purchase instalments every month, but he should make enough profit to be able to meet the instalments. Had William used hire purchase, then the balance sheet at 1 June would have read as shown in Figure 8.4.

	£
Capital	20,000
Medium-/long-term liability	
Hire purchase	7,000
Capital employed	27,000
Employment of capital	
Fixed assets	18,000
Working capital	9,000
	27,000

Figure 8.4

With the extra £7,000 in the bank, the working capital at 30 June would have been as shown in Figure 8.5.

Current assets	£
Stocks	9,000
Debtors	1,000
Bank	8,000
Total Current Assets	18,000
Less: Current Liability	9,000
Working capital	9,000

Figure 8.5

The current ratio would then be 2:1 and the acid test ratio 1:1.

A rule of thumb when starting a new business is that the amount owing to suppliers should not become greater than the amount of the working capital.

What changes the amount of working capital?

Once a business starts operating, the amount of working capital keeps changing.

- *Making a profit will increase* the working capital. If you buy a pair of shoes for £30 and sell them for £50, you have made a profit of £20 which increases your working capital by £20.
- *Making a loss will reduce* the working capital.
- *Selling fixed assets increases* the working capital. Nearly all businesses have equipment they are not using and could sell. The cash realised increases the working capital. Perhaps you have a branch or division you could sell?
- *Borrowing money on a medium-/long-term basis increases* the working capital. If you arrange a loan of £15,000 repayable over the next three years, and pay the loan into the bank, the working capital will increase by £10,000 (£5,000 of the loan is a current liability).
- *Repaying loans reduces* the working capital. As you repay the loan of £15,000, each repayment reduces the bank balance and the working capital.
- *New equity increases* the working capital. If a new block of 20,000 shares is issued, at an issue price of £1 each, £20,000 will be paid into the bank, and the working capital will increase by £20,000.

When the amount of working capital stays the same

- When we pay creditors, the balance at the bank is reduced, and current liabilities are also reduced, so the amount of working capital stays the same.
- When we buy stock on credit, stock is increased and current liabilities are also increased, so the amount of working capital stays the same.
- When we borrow money by overdrawing at the bank, working capital stays the same *provided* we use the money borrowed to pay creditors. The current liability – overdraft – increases, and creditors decrease. But if we use the overdraft to buy fixed assets or pay off loans, then working capital will be reduced.

Getting the most out of each pound of working capital

The secret is to make every pound of working capital spin round as quickly as possible.

Stock

The rate at which stock spins round, 'turns over', is called the stock turn ratio. We divide the sales for the year by the average stock (at selling price). The average stock is the stock at the beginning and end of the year, added together and divided by 2. (For a more accurate figure, add up the stocks at each month-end, through the year, and divide by 12.)

Here is the stock ratio of Smart Clothes and Co:

$$£$$

Sales for the year	$\dfrac{150{,}000}{50{,}000}$ = 3 times
Average stock (selling price)	

The stock turned over three times during the year.

If Smart Clothes and Co could make the stock turn over *four* times a year, then the average stock needed would be a quarter less, that is £50,000 less one quarter: £37,500. The stock turn would then be:

Sales for the year	$\dfrac{150{,}000}{37{,}500}$ = 4 times
Average stock	

If stock was reduced to £37,500, then there would be £12,500 more in the bank. Or the stock of £12,500 saved could be used to open another branch.

How do we make stock turn over faster?

By planning stock levels: Smart Clothes and Co keep records of sales and stocks, in units, divided into categories. One category is summer dresses. During the winter, the dress buyer works out a plan (see Figure 8.6) for summer dresses for the next summer season.

	DRESSES (Units)
Planned sales for the season	3,000
Add: planned closing stock	1,100
Total required for the season	4,100
Less: actual opening stock	900
Total dresses to buy	3,200

Figure 8.6

This plan gives a stock turn of:

$$\frac{\text{Sales}}{\text{Average stock}} \qquad \frac{3,000}{\frac{1}{2} (1,100 + 900)} = 3 \text{ times}$$

The buyer gives the plan to the merchandise controller. The merchandise controller thinks the planned sales figure is too low and he and the buyer agree to increase planned sales to 3,200 dresses. The merchandise controller also insists that planned closing stock of 1,100 is far too high. They eventually agree that the planned closing stock should be 700.

The revised plan is shown in Figure 8.7.

	DRESSES
	(Units)
Planned sales	3,200
Add: planned closing stock	700
	3,900
Less: actual opening stock	900
Total dresses to buy	3,000

Figure 8.7

The new plan gives a stock turn of:

$$\frac{\text{Sales}}{\text{Average stock}} \qquad \frac{3,200}{\frac{1}{2} (700 + 900)} = 4 \text{ times}$$

The revised plan increases planned stock turn from 3 to 4 times.

As the season progresses, actual sales will be compared with the plan. If the actual sales look like being less than the plan, orders for dresses can be cut back to ensure that the actual stock is not greater than the planned closing stock.

Similar plans can be made for all kinds of stock – raw materials, spare parts and so on.

Here is another way of thinking about stock turn. If, from a stock of 2 dresses, you sell 4 dresses a month, then stock turned over 2 times. If, with the same stock of 2 dresses, you sell 6 dresses a month, then stock turn is 3 times. With a stock turn of 3, you are making 6 lots of profit in a month on the 6 dresses you sell, compared with 4 lots of profit. So the money invested in the stock of dresses is now 50 per cent more productive. Also, with the stock turn of 3, the dresses are hanging in the shop for a shorter time – reducing losses from the dresses going out of fashion, getting shop-soiled and so on.

The stock/debtor 'trade-off'

By giving generous discounts, customers can be encouraged to buy goods earlier than usual. In this way stock is converted into debtors. By reducing stocks, stock turn is improved. By increasing debtors, the acid test ratio is improved. If the customers take immediate delivery of the goods, the costs of holding stock – storage, deterioration and the like – will be borne by the customer.

Debtors

The object of credit management is to be paid in accordance with your own terms.

If all debtors pay on due date, then the working capital used for the debtors is being used efficiently.

A good way of measuring this efficiency is to work out the average number of days the debtors have been outstanding. The calculation is:

$$\frac{\text{Average debtors}}{\text{Credit sales for the year}} \times 365 \text{ days}$$

For example, the balance of debtors outstanding in the books of Smart Clothes and Co at the beginning and the end of the year, added together and divided by 2, is £8,000.

The credit sales for the year were £73,000.

The average number of days the debtors were outstanding (counting from the last day of the month in which each sale took place) is:

$$\frac{8,000}{73,000} \quad \text{x} \quad \frac{365}{1} = 40 \text{ days}$$

Smart Clothes terms are 'payment within 30 days of statement'. As the average time before payment is received is in fact 40 days, you can see that many customers are not paying on time.

The important thing about all ratios is comparison. Last year, the average number of days the Smart Clothes debtors were outstanding was 48 days. So this year's ratio of 40 days is an improvement.

Success in meeting the management objective of 'payment in accordance with our terms' depends on:

- *Correctly assessing the credit character of the customer:* credit character is judged from age, job, whether married, whether a house owner, and on credit references from the customer's other suppliers and the bank. The credit character of a company is assessed from its credit references, the amount of share capital issued and the credit characters of the directors. Bankers and other lenders will also want to see the company's balance sheet.

- *Follow up when payment is not made on time:* wherever possible this should be by personal approach, rather than a letter, or form letter.

Collateral

Banks and other lenders nearly always ask for collateral. Collateral is security – like the mortgage of a property, or a guarantee from a wealthy relative – which can be realised if the debtor fails to pay. Realising a collateral security can often take a long time, so obtaining collateral does not help in ensuring payment on due date.

Cash flow budget

Good working capital management depends on the company preparing a cash flow budget for the year to come. The idea is simple.

For each month of the year an estimate is made of:

$£$

Estimated bank balance at the beginning of the month...X
Add: expected receipts for the month – sales, debtor payments, borrowings, etc X
Less: expected payments for the month – creditor payments, wages and salaries, rent, loan repayments, tax, dividends, buying assets, etc X
Gives: estimated bank balance at the end of the month...X

The budget will give early warning of future cash flow problems, so that plans can be made to meet problems.

As part of preparing the cash flow budget, decisions will be needed on stock levels, investment in fixed assets, credit policy and anticipated debtor levels for each month of the year. Also forecasts must be made of expected sales and expenses month by month.

By good planning, a business can operate comfortably on less working capital. Good planning therefore releases working capital for expansion.

Good financial management has a powerful effect upon the financial strength and growth prospects of a company. Good financial management is an 'asset' which appears nowhere in the balance sheet, and yet is one of the most effective assets of the company.

Other 'assets' not revealed by a balance sheet include money spent on the training of staff, the value of skilled personnel at all levels, and money spent on developing products and systems.

Self-check

At 31 March 19XX, DL Ltd had the following assets and liabilities: Stocks £125,000, Debtors £25,000, Creditors £30,000, Overdraft £20,000, Land and buildings £75,000, Mortgage loan £50,000.

1. The current assets totalled:
   (a) £125,000 (b) £225,000 (c) £150,000 (d) £170,000
2. The current liabilities totalled:
   (a) £50,000 (b) £30,000 (c) £80,000 (d) £20,000
3. The current ratio was:
   (a) 1:3 (b) 3:1 (c) 5:1 (d) 1:5
4. The acid test ratio was:
   (a) 0.5:1 (b) 5:1 (c) 1:2 (d) 3:1
5. KR Ltd's stock at retail prices at 1 January 19XX was £9,000 and at 31 December 19XX was £5,000. The sales for 19XX totalled £14,000. The stock turn for the year was:
   (a) 5 (b) 1 (c) 2 (d) 20
6. A current ratio of 3:1 suggests that the business:
   (a) Has sufficient working capital;
   (b) Has insufficient working capital;
   (c) Has too much stock;
   (d) Can pay its creditors on time.
7. An acid test ratio of 0.5:1 indicates that the business:
   (a) Has sufficient working capital;
   (b) Has insufficient working capital;
   (c) May have difficulty in paying its creditors on time;
   (d) Has too much stock.
8. Which one of the following factors does *not* increase working capital?
   (a) Profit;
   (b) Borrowing money on a medium-/long-term basis;
   (c) Buying a new fixed asset;
   (d) Issuing more shares.
9. The object of credit management is:
   (a) To increase sales;

(b) To have no bad debts;
(c) To be paid in accordance with your terms;
(d) To have an efficient follow-up system.
10. To improve stock turn we must:
(a) Increase sales;
(b) Reduce purchases;
(c) Plan sales and stock levels;
(d) Reduce stocks.

Answers
1c, 2a, 3b, 4a, 5c, 6a, 7c, 8c, 9c, 10c.

Chapter 9

The Limited Liability Company

Many countries have a Companies Act based on the first British Companies Act of 1862, and the far-reaching amendments made to that Act over the past century. The Companies Acts in various countries differ, but the basic principles are the same.

The owners of the company are the shareholders. The shareholders have invested money in the company and received share certificates from the company secretary. The company itself is a legal entity, distinct from the shareholders. If the company becomes involvent and is liquidated, the shareholders will lose most or all of the money they have invested in shares, but they will not be personally responsible for the unpaid debts of the company. The liability of the shareholders (who are also called 'members') is therefore limited to the amount they have invested (or promised to invest) in shares. The creditors of a liquidated company cannot ask members to pay them any amounts still owing by the company.

(People sometimes think that the members of a company are liable, on a liquidation, to pay in the amount of the *authorised* share capital of the company. This is not so. Their liability is limited to the amount they have actually invested – or promised to invest – in shares, which is usually an amount less than the authorised share capital.)

Establishing a company

Memorandum of Association
A company is created by the promoters (the people setting up the company), who employ a lawyer to draw up a constitution for the company, called the Memorandum and Articles of Association.

The Memorandum of Association includes:

- The name of the company;

- The company's objects; for example, 'to operate a quarry';
- A statement that the liability of members is limited to their investment (or promised investment) in shares;
- The nominal value of a share (the *face* value printed on a share certificate) eg £1, 50 pence, 10 pence, etc, also called the *par value*;
- The authorised share capital – that is, the maximum share capital the company is allowed to issue.

The Memorandum is signed by the first shareholders, bringing them into 'association' as founders and shareholders of the company.

Articles of Association

The Articles of Association are very detailed rules about the inner workings of a company. The articles cover such matters as how directors are appointed, meetings conducted, and the like. The directors are appointed by the shareholders to manage the company. With small companies, the shareholders and the directors are often the same people, but even so each person has two separate roles – shareholder and director.

Incorporation

When the lawyer has completed the Memorandum and Articles of Asssociation, he deposits them with the Registrar of Companies, together with a fee. If all is in order, the Registrar will issue a Certificate of Incorporation, which is the birth certificate of the company. The company can then begin to function.

The word 'incorporate' means to 'make into a body'. With a company, the body is a legal body – a bundle of papers. The shareholders will then appoint the directors to be the hands, eyes and brains of the company.

A company is 'born' when it is incorporated. It will only 'die' when it is wound up. The shareholders will die, but their company goes on living. This is an advantage of family-owned companies: the business does not cease to exist when the majority shareholder dies. The shares can be passed on to the heirs.

Public and private companies

Companies can either be public companies or private companies. In Britain, public companies have the abbreviation 'plc' after the company name. Private companies simply have the word 'Limited' (or Ltd) after the name.

In other countries the word 'Incorporated' is sometimes used after the company name, instead of 'Limited'.

In some countries, private companies are identified by the words 'Private Limited' or 'Proprietary Limited'.

The differences between a public and a private company are small. A private company may not offer its shares to the public, but it is free of some of the legal requirements of public companies.

The shares in many public companies are not traded on the Stock Exchange but may be bought and sold through stockbrokers and finance houses.

A Stock Exchange is simply a market-place. It is like a vegetable market, except that instead of trading in vegetables, it is shares which are being bought and sold. The daily price at which a share is bought and sold is called the *quoted price*.

If a company wishes to have its shares listed on a Stock Exchange, it applies to the Stock Exchange Council. The Stock Exchange Council in each country is a private body – it is not set up under the Companies Act. But the operations of the Stock Exchange are sometimes regulated by law.

Conduct and structure

Annual general meeting

The Companies Act stipulates a compulsory annual general meeting of shareholders. At this meeting, the shareholders:

- Approve the balance sheet and accounts for the year. These statements are prepared by the directors for presentation to the shareholders.
- Approve any dividend recommended by the directors and transfers to reserve (which we look at later).
- Appoint directors for the forthcoming year.
- Appoint auditors, who check the accounts on behalf of the shareholders.

Share capital

A basic rule of company law is that the money invested in shares – the 'issued share capital' – is the *permanent* capital of the company. If the company becomes insolvent the share capital constitutes a pool from which the creditors can be paid because, if the company is wound up, the creditors are paid out first, and the shareholders last. Shareholders only receive the cash remaining, if any, *after* the creditors have been paid. A large amount of issued share capital, therefore, gives confidence to creditors of the company.

The issued share capital is called *non-distributable*.

Redemption of shares

Under the UK Companies Act, however, it is possible for a UK company to refund ('redeem') shares, or to buy its own shares back from shareholders.

But the permanent capital of the company must be maintained, despite shares being repaid.

(The advantages of a company being able to buy its own shares include: buy out dissident shareholders; buy back employee shares if the employee leaves the company; pay out the estate of a deceased shareholder; use up surplus company cash; by reducing shares in issue, increase profit per share and dividend ratios.)

The permanent capital can be maintained in two ways:

1. New shares may be issued to replace the redeemed shares.
2. By creating a capital redemption reserve. Most companies do not pay out ('distribute') *all* their profits as a dividend.

   Companies usually leave part of the profit in the business to finance growth. The profits held back are called *retained profits*. Retained profits are, however, still distributable – should the directors and shareholders wish to pay out the retained profit.

   Retained profits can be used to replace the permanent capital paid out as a share redemption. To do this, an amount equal to the nominal value of the redeemed shares is transferred from the retained profits to an account called the *capital redemption reserve*. The capital redemption reserve is a capital reserve and, in terms of the Companies Act, is *non*-distributable. The capital redemption reserve is therefore part of the permanent capital of the company and replaces the capital lost when the shares were redeemed.

Premium on redemption

Very often shares are redeemed or bought back at a price greater than nominal value. The extra amount paid is called a premium on redemption. This premium is normally paid from retained profits.

Ordinary shares

There are different classes of shares. The most common class is called *ordinary shares*. The ordinary shareholders normally have one vote for each share they hold. The annual general meeting of the company is

Example
In this company, shares with a nominal value of £10,000 were refunded to shareholders.

Before Redemption	£	After Redemption	£
Share capital	30,000	Share capital	20,000
		Capital redemption reserve	10,000
Non-distributable capital	30,000	Non-distributable capital	30,000
Retained profits	20,000	Retained profits	10,000
Equity	50,000	Equity	40,000

Figure 9.1

Note that although the *equity* has fallen from £50,000 to £40,000 owing to the refund of share capital, the *non-distributable* capital remains the same – £30,000.

therefore controlled by the people with the majority of ordinary shares. The company's profits belong to the ordinary shareholders, who receive part of the profits each year as a dividend.

A *dividend* is the amount of profit paid to the shareholders in respect of each of the shares they hold. For example, if the nominal value of each share is £1, the dividend may be described as '15 pence per share' or 15 per cent. If profits are high, ordinary dividends increase. If the company has a loss, no ordinary dividend will be paid.

Preference shares
Preference shares are very different from ordinary shares. They carry no vote. The preference shareholders receive a fixed dividend each year, and they do not usually share in the profits apart from their fixed dividend. The holder of a 12 per cent preference share with a nominal value of £1 will be paid an annual dividend of 12 pence.

The preference dividend is a first charge on the profits, before the ordinary dividend. Should the company be liquidated, the preference shareholders have first claim on the funds of the company, after the creditors and lenders have been paid. The ordinary shareholders are the last in the payment queue.

Preference shares are usually 'cumulative'. This means that if there is insufficient profit available for the payment of the preference dividend, then two years' dividend will be paid next year (provided profits are then available).

Preference shares are sometimes called 'participating'. This means that the shareholders are entitled to an additional amount of dividend if company profits reach an agreed level.

Preference shares are not an exciting investment, because usually they do not benefit from growth in company profits. However, they are sometimes convertible into ordinary shares.

The profit and loss account

By law, a company must attach to its balance sheet a profit and loss account for the year ended on the date of the balance sheet. Under the UK Companies Act, the profit and loss account will give, in essence, the information shown in Figure 9.2.

BM Ltd
Profit and Loss Account for the year ended 30 June 1998

	£
Sales (also called TURNOVER)	2,797,000
Less: COST OF SALES (the cost of the goods sold)	1,862,000
GROSS PROFIT (the total income from trading)	935,000
Add: other income received	31,000
Total income	966,000
Less: DISTRIBUTIVE AND ADMINISTRATIVE EXPENSES	510,000
NET PROFIT	456,000

Figure 9.2

Exceptional or extraordinary items of income or expense will be shown as separate items in the profit and loss account. The 'earnings' of the company for the year will be the net profit *before* adding or deducting the exceptional or extraordinary items. An extraordinary item is one that arises from outside the company's ordinary activities. An exceptional item is one that is within the company's ordinary activities but is abnormal because of its large amount. For example, writing off a bad debt in the books of a trading company would not be 'extraordinary', but if the amount was proportionately huge, then it would be 'exceptional'. The idea behind disclosing these extraordinary and exceptional items is to make comparisons of trading results, with previous years or other companies, possible.

Appropriation

After the figure of net profit, the directors show how the profit will be *appropriated* – that is, distributed.

- The first appropriation is company taxation.
- The second appropriation is the preference dividend.
- The third appropriation is any transfer to general reserve.
- The last appropriation is the recommended dividend payable to the ordinary shareholders.

General reserve

The full amount of profit is often not available in cash, because the cash resulting from making a profit has already been partly used up in expansion – larger stocks, new equipment, new branches and so on. If the cash represented by the profit is not in the bank, the company is unable to pay the entire profit as a cash dividend to the shareholders.

To show the shareholders that the entire profit is not available as a dividend, many companies transfer part of the profit from the profit and loss account to a separate account called a general reserve. If, at some future time, cash becomes available to pay a dividend, then the company can transfer the profit from the general reserve back to the profit and loss account – and declare a dividend. The general reserve appears in the balance sheet as part of the equity, because it is profit which belongs to the shareholders. A general reserve is distributable – if cash is available.

Sometimes companies will transfer profit to a general reserve even if cash *is* available for a dividend. The transfer may be made because the directors plan to use the profit for future expansion.

Some balance sheet readers – perhaps trade union officials – suppose that, because a company has large revenue reserves, it must be in a position to pay higher wages. Is this so?

The general reserve, plus any retained profit remaining at the bottom of the profit and loss account, are together called the *revenue reserve*.

Figure 9.3 shows the appropriation section of the profit and loss account:

BM Ltd

	£
Net profit for the year	456,000
Less: company tax	228,000
Profit after taxation	228,000
Less: recommended transfer to general reserve	150,000
Profit available for distribution	78,000
Less: recommended ordinary dividend of 25p a share	70,000
Retained profit	8,000

Figure 9.3

Figure 9.4 shows the equity section of the balance sheet for BM Ltd.

BM Ltd
Balance Sheet at 30 June 19XX

	£	£	£
Issued share capital			280,000
280,000 ordinary shares			
Revenue reserve (retained profit)			
General reserve:			
At 1 July 19XX		200,000	
Add: transfer for the year		150,000	
Retained profit:		350,000	
At 1 July 19XX	15,000		
Retained profit for the year	8,000	23,000	373,000
			653,000

Figure 9.4

Remember, the revenue reserve is retained profit and is distributable provided sufficient cash to pay a dividend is available.

The growth of equity

A company builds up its equity and financial strength by holding back profit. Let us follow the fortunes of AS Ltd, a newly formed company (Figure 9.5).

AS Ltd
Balance Sheet – Year 1

	£
Shares issued	40,000
Fixed assets (land and buildings)	28,000
Working capital	12,000
	40,000

Figure 9.5

The company started with shares issued of £40,000. Trading had not yet begun.

Year 2

The company ended year 2 with retained profit of £8,000. Also during year 2, a further 10,000 shares had been issued. The new shareholders had to pay £1.20 for each £1 share. The directors could charge the premium of 20 pence because the company now had good prospects, and the shares had become a good investment.

The *share premium*, like the share capital, is non-distributable, and is therefore shown as capital reserve (Figure 9.6).

Balance Sheet – Year 2

	£
Shares issued	50,000
Capital reserve	
Share premium	2,000
Non-distributable capital	52,000
Revenue reserve	
Retained profit	8,000
Equity	60,000

Fixed assets (land and buildings)		28,000
Working capital		32,000
		60,000

Figure 9.6

Year 3

In the third year, the directors decided to revalue the land and buildings. A value increase of £12,000 is added to the fixed assets, and this 'paper profit' of £12,000 was added to equity – as part of the capital reserve. The paper profit is shown as a capital reserve because the profit is not normally distributable until the property is sold, and the profit is realised in cash (Figure 9.7).

Balance Sheet – Year 3

		£
Shares issued		50,000
Capital reserve		
Share premium	2,000	
Revaluation	12,000	14,000
Non-distributable capital		64,000
Revenue reserve:		
Retained profit from year 2	8,000	
Add: year 3	6,000	14,000
		78,000
Equity		
Fixed assets (land and buildings)		40,000
Working capital		38,000
		78,000

Figure 9.7

Year 4

In year 4, the directors recommended to the members that the capital reserve be used to finance a bonus issue of shares to the shareholders. Each shareholder received, free of charge, 28 extra shares for each 100 shares he or she held.

Balance Sheet – Year 4

	£	£
Shares issued		64,000
Capital reserve		
Carried forward	14,000	
Less: bonus issue	14,000	–
Non-distributable capital		64,000
Revenue reserve		
Retained profit – from year 3	14,000	
Add: year 4	6,000	20,000
Equity		84,000
Fixed assets (land and buildings)		40,000
Working capital		44,000
		84,000

Figure 9.8

Year 5

In the fifth year, the directors recommended that, out of the revenue reserve, £9,000 be used to finance the issue of a further batch of bonus shares. This issue increased the non-distributable capital by £9,000, which strengthened the appearance of the balance sheet in the eyes of the lenders to the company. Of course, the bonus issue also meant that the £9,000 of profit, which might have been paid out as a dividend, was now irretrievably locked in. However, the cash represented by this profit was permanently committed as part of the working capital needed for the smooth operation of the company.

Balance Sheet – Year 5

	£	£
Shares issued		73,000
Revenue reserve		
Retained profit carried forward	20,000	
Less: bonus issue	9,000	11,000
Equity		84,000

Fixed assets (land and buildings)	40,000
Working capital	44,000
	84,000

Figure 9.9

Debenture loans

Debentures are entirely different from shares. The word debenture is from a Latin phrase *debentur mihi* – 'these are owed to me'. A debenture loan is money loaned to a company, and acknowledged by issuing debenture certificates to lenders. The loan carries interest at a fixed rate, and is repayable at a future date.

The advantage of debenture certificates is that the lender can sell his or her certificate to someone else, should he or she wish to liquidate his investment before the redemption date.

Debenture loans are not part of equity and they carry no vote. They are medium-/long-term borrowings. The debenture interest is an expense of the company like any other expense. Often the debenture loan is secured by the company mortgaging some of the company's assets to a trustee for the debenture holders. Then, if the interest is not paid, or the company becomes insolvent, the mortgaged assets can be sold, and the debenture holders paid out from the proceeds. (Debentures not so secured may be described as 'unsecured loan stock'.)

Sometimes debentures are convertible into ordinary shares.

Limited company status

The advantages

Small businesses are often in the legal form of 'sole trader' or partnership. Sole traders, and partnerships, are unincorporated, and the owners and partners are personally responsible for all the debts of the business. The transformation of a sole trader or partnership business into a limited company gives the owners limited liability but there are other, perhaps more important, benefits:

(a) When a partnership is incorporated, the Articles of Association can include provision for the withdrawal of a partner. Any partner wishing to withdraw may offer his shares to the remaining shareholders at a valuation fixed by the auditors, and payable by the remaining shareholders over a number of years plus interest. This arrangement avoids the firm breaking up.

(b) In a family business, the Articles can provide that while the shares are equally distributed among the children, the family member actually managing the business can be given superior voting power on matters relating to the running of the business.

(c) The shareholders can invite suitable experienced outsiders to serve as directors. The involvement of an outside director may only amount to a few hours a year, and the fee payable may be small, but the advice, knowledge and contacts of such a director can be very valuable to what may otherwise be a one-man business.

The disadvantages

These include the legal, secretarial and audit costs. Taxation payable by a company may be greater or smaller than that for an unincorporated business. It all depends on the tax law in your country. Check with a taxation specialist.

Self-check

True or False?

1. Revenue reserves are distributable. T F
2. Share premiums are non-distributable. T F
3. Profits from 'increases' in the value of assets are non-distributable. T F
4. Preference shareholders normally have a vote at a general meeting. T F
5. A company belongs to its directors. T F
6. The shares in a public company are always quoted on the Stock Exchange. T F
7. Debentures are part of equity. T F
8. Directors' fees and salaries are an appropriation of profits. T F
9. Profits from increases in the value of assets are not normally distributable until the assets are sold. T F
10. The first appropriation of profit is income tax. T F
11. The shares in some public companies are quoted on a Stock Exchange. T F
12. A general reserve often shows the amount of profit set aside because cash is not available for its distribution. T F
13. Debentures are loans, and are not part of equity. T F
14. Converting revenue reserves into bonus shares increases the credit worthiness of the company. T F
15. Directors' fees and salaries are an administrative expense of the company. T F

Answers
1T, 2T, 3F, 4F, 5F, 6F, 7F, 8F, 9T, 10T, 11T, 12T, 13T, 14T, 15T.

Chapter 10
Group Accounts

Your interest may be in the balance sheets of companies quoted on a Stock Exchange. Quoted companies are often the holding company of a group of subsidiary companies.

For example, a holding company in the retail trade may have separate subsidiary companies trading in fashionwear, furniture, footwear and so on. A subsidiary company is:

1. a company in which the holding company has more than half the shares, or
2. a company in which the holding company has less than half the shares but has the power to appoint the directors of the subsidiary.

Consolidated (group) balance sheets

The Companies Act requires a holding company to publish, together with its own balance sheet, a consolidated balance sheet.

The consolidated balance sheet (also called the group balance sheet) is arrived at by adding the balance sheets of the holding company and its various subsidiaries together.* For example, shown in Figure 10.1 are the balance sheets of Holding Ltd, and its subsidiary, Subsid Ltd, at 30 June 19XX.

When the two balance sheets are added together, the investment of £100,000 in the balance sheet of Holding Ltd is cancelled out against the equity in Subsid Ltd, and the group balance sheet reads as shown in Figure 10.2.

* Although the principle of consolidation is simple, the accounting procedures are very complex.

Holding Ltd Balance Sheet		Subsid Ltd Balance Sheet	
	£		£
Equity	250,000	Equity	100,000
Debentures	90,000	Debentures	30,000
Capital employed	340,000	Capital employed	130,000
Fixed assets	80,000	Fixed assets	60,000
Investment in Subsid Ltd	100,000		
Working capital	160,000	Working capital	70,000
	340,000		130,000

Figure 10.1

**Holding Ltd
Group Balance Sheet**

	£
Equity	250,000
Debentures	120,000
Capital employed	370,000
Fixed assets	140,000
Working capital	230,000
	370,000

Figure 10.2

Often there are minority shareholders with shares in the subsidiary. Supposing Holding Ltd had invested only £70,000 in Subsid Ltd, instead of £100,000, the remaining £30,000 of equity in Subsid Ltd remaining in the hands of minority shareholders. In this case, when the balance sheets are added together the investment of £70,000 will not cancel out the equity of £100,000. We will be left with equity in the subsidiary of £30,000. This equity of £30,000 appears in the group balance sheet as the equity held by minorities, as shown in Figure 10.3. (We will add the reduction of £30,000 in Holding Ltd's investment to working capital – the £30,000 would still be in the bank.)

Holding Ltd
Group Balance Sheet

	£
Equity	250,000
MINORITY INTEREST	30,000
Debentures	120,000
Capital employed	400,000
Fixed assets	140,000
Working capital	260,000
	400,000

Figure 10.3

In our example, the equity of the group – £250,000 – is the same as the equity of Holding Ltd. But as the years go by, the subsidiaries accumulate retained profits which are added to equity in the group accounts. The profits of the subsidiaries are part of the earnings – and equity – of the group.

You will find that the annual report of a holding company usually includes the holding company's balance sheet, as well as the group balance sheet. The holding company balance sheet can usually be ignored – it is published mainly to comply with the Companies Act. Your interest will be in the group balance sheet.

Associated companies

These are companies which are not subsidiaries, but in which the holding company holds at least 20 per cent of the shares and influences the management of the associate.

Because associated companies are not subsidiaries, they are not included in the group consolidation. But investment in associates can be a very important part of a company's activities.

For instance, KL Contractors Ltd, a civil engineering company, is a one-third partner in a company called Consortium Ltd, formed to handle a huge engineering contract. This type of joint venture is increasingly common.

Consortium Ltd makes large profits which are retained and ploughed back into the company. It is important for KL Contractors Ltd to be able to show in its profit and loss account and balance sheet its portion of

Consortium's retained profit. Otherwise, the increasing value of KL Contractors' investment in Consortium will not be visible to KL's shareholders.

The investing company's share of the retained profit in an associate, from the date of the holding company's investment, is often shown in the investing company's balance sheet by adding the profit to the investing company's equity, and also to its investment in the associate as shown in Figure 10.4.

KL Contractors Ltd
Balance Sheet: 31 December

	£	£
Equity		500,000
Add: share of profit to date in Consortium Ltd		55,000
Total equity		555,000
Investment in associated company, Consortium Ltd:		
Cost	250,000	
Add: share of profit to date	55,000	305,000
Other assets		250,000
		555,000

Figure 10.4

Self-check

True or False?

1. To be a subsidiary company, the holding company must hold at least half the shares in it.   T F
2. In group accounts, the figure for assets is the total of all the assets in the group added together.   T F
3. The item 'minority interests' in a group balance sheet represents the portion of equity in subsidiary companies belonging to outside shareholders.   T F
4. To be a subsidiary company, the holding company must hold at

least half the shares in a subsidiary company or control the
board of the subsidiary.   T F
5. In group balance sheets, the equity consists of the equities of the
   holding company and the subsidiaries added together.   T F
6. The investment in an associated company is usually shown in
   the investing company's balance sheet at cost plus profit.   T F

Answers

1F, 2T, 3T, 4T, 5F, 6T.

Chapter 11
Balance Sheet and Investors' Ratios

Balance sheet ratios fall into three groups:

- Gearing ratios
- Working capital ratios
- Efficiency ratios.

Over the years, balance sheet analysts have developed many different ratios. In this chapter we will review a small selection of ratios which will help to give a general picture of a business. We have already introduced some of these ratios; others are new. Remember that ratios often mislead. They are best regarded as an *aide-mémoire*, a means of drawing your attention to certain important comparisons, and to make you think.

Gearing ratios

- Equity as a percentage of capital employed. (See page 46.)
- Interest-bearing debt ratio.

Interest-bearing debt includes medium-/long-term loans on which interest is payable, such as debentures and mortgage loans. It also includes interest-bearing borrowings included with the current liabilities, like an overdraft.

We express the total interest-bearing debt as a percentage of equity. Some authorities say the ratio should not be more than 60 per cent. But it all depends on the circumstances of the business. This ratio has the benefit of making one think about how much of the liabilities are interest-free. A high proportion of interest-free financing (like creditors) might indicate good financial management. Comparison with other companies in the same industry is useful.

Working capital ratios (see Chapter 8)

- Current ratio
- Acid test ratio
- Stock turn.

Efficiency ratios

Percentage increase in before-tax profits
Calculate the percentage increase of before-tax profits, year by year, over the past five years. Are the increases greater than the rate of inflation? Is the company showing a steady increase in profits (adjusted for inflation) year after year?

Return on equity (also called return on investment)
After-tax profit as a percentage of equity: comparisons of return on equity, between companies, are often difficult because each company has its own policy on providing for deferred tax (which affects both profits and equity), and on the revaluation of fixed assets (which affects the amount of equity). Whether or not associated company profits are shown also affects the percentage (see pages 77-8).

Trading profit (before tax and interest) as a percentage of turnover
This ratio gives a good picture of the operating efficiency of a business. The percentage should be compared with that for competitors, as well as with previous years.

Trading profit (before tax and interest) as a percentage of the total assets
Exclude any goodwill from the assets: a company may have a high percentage of profit to turnover, but when the same profit is expressed as a percentage of all the asssets used, the percentage may be lower than that of competitors. This suggests that assets are being used wastefully.

A point to look for is whether the company is using borrowed money for which it is paying a higher rate of interest than the percentage return on total assets.

The percentage balance sheet

This is a useful way of directing your thoughts to changes in assets and liabilities this year compared with last year, and comparing the asset/ liability structure of the company with that of competitors.

Take the assets and liabilities from the balance sheet and set them out in two columns – assets and liabilities. Then express each asset and liability as a percentage of the total, as shown in Figure 11.1.

OW Ltd
Assets and Liabilities at 31 March 19XX

Liabilities	£	%	Assets	£	%
Equity	56,000	40.6	Fixed assets	97,000	70.3
Medium-/ long-term			Current assets		
borrowings	37,000	26.8	Stock	36,000	26.1
Deferred tax	18,000	13.0	Debtors/cash/		3.6
			bills	5,000	
Current liabilities	27,000	19.6	Total current assets	41,000	29.7
TOTAL LIABILITIES	138,000	100.0	TOTAL ASSETS	138,000	100.0

Figure 11.1

Debt repayment ratio

How long would it take for the company to repay its medium-/long-term debt if, in theory, it repaid the debt from retained profits? To find out, divide the medium-/long-term debt by the amount of profit the company normally retains each year. The answer is the number of years it would take to repay the debt. Compare this number of years with the *actual* repayment period – which will be shown in notes to the balance sheet. This 'debt repayment ratio' is very theoretical, but it will help you to think about how the company will repay its debt. This ratio is sometimes called the 'insolvency ratio'. But as a prediction of insolvency, the ratio should be treated with circumspection.

Statement of sources and applications of funds

A useful insight into the changes in a company's finances over the years can be obtained from the statement of sources and applications of funds. This statement and its uses are described in Appendix E.

An example

As Appendix D we print the profit and loss account and balance sheet for Marks & Spencer plc, one of Britain's finest retail chains, with an analysis using the ratios we have described.

Using investors' ratios

These ratios are of interest to investors buying quoted shares on a Stock Exchange. The ratios should be compared with the previous year's ratio, and with the same ratio for other companies in the same field of activity.

Dividend cover

Annual dividend, divided into after-tax profits for the year. Companies often retain about half the profit to cover expansion and inflation and pay out the other half as a dividend. This would give a dividend cover of 2 (after-tax profit is twice the dividend).

Dividend yield

The annual dividend per share as a percentage of the market price of the share. In the United Kingdom this is usually calculated on gross dividend (see Glossary).

Earnings per share

After-tax profits for the year divided by the number of shares in issue.

Earnings yield

After-tax profits per share as a percentage of the market price of the share.

Net worth per share

The equity of the company (which is the same amount as the net worth of the company) divided by the number of shares in issue. Compare this figure with the market price of a share.

Is the market price greater than the net worth of a share or less?

If the net worth per share is considerably greater than the market value, a speculator might buy up shares in the company until he has a controlling interest. Or he could publish an offer to all the shareholders to buy their shares at a price attractive to them (called a *takeover bid*). Having gained control of the company, the speculator may then cause the company to sell its assets, creating profits and cash in the company which can then be used for the payment of dividends or for financing further takeover bids.

The policy of the company on deferred taxation and asset revaluation directly affects this ratio.

Price/earnings ratio

This is the market price of a share divided by the earnings per share.

If the price of the share is high in proportion to the earnings, then the PE ratio will be a high number – like 20. Shares which have good growth prospects will usually have a high PE ratio.

A low PE ratio – like 8 – could result from poor earnings, or because, for some reason, the shares are underpriced.

Fortunes have been made by investors who have investigated low PE shares and invested in shares which are unreasonably underpriced. This type of investment requires careful assessment of balance sheets, especially net worth per share. (A visit to the company concerned can be most helpful.)

Valuing a share

Shares in public companies, which are not quoted, are often bought and sold through stockbrokers. The PE ratio can be used to value a share which is not quoted on the Stock Exchange, the Unlisted Securities Market or the Third Market. For example, you are thinking of buying shares in an unquoted manufacturing company. The earnings per share are 10 pence. The PE ratio for quoted manufacturing companies ranges from 5 (low) to 15 (high) with a mean of about 11. Multiply the earnings per share by those ratios and you have a price range of:

Low	£0.50 per share
High	£1.50 per share
Mean	£1.10 per share

Next you have to study the company balance sheet, and also find out something about the company's prospects, and the quality of the company's management. Then you can decide whether the correct price for the shares falls into the low, high or medium bracket. Bear in mind that it is not easy to sell an unquoted share because there is no regular market. Therefore the value of an unquoted share will be less than that of an equivalent, quoted share.

You must also find out the company's dividend policy. What proportion of the annual earnings are paid out as a dividend?

Q. But surely the dividends the investor will actually receive are all that matters in valuing a share?

A. Of course, the dividends paid are vital – no one wants to invest in a share which gives them little or no dividend. But the amount of earnings *retained* is also of great importance. Company X and company Y both pay the same annual dividend. The dividend cover of X is 2 and Y, 3. The shares in Y will be a better investment because for every £1 paid out as dividend, Y is retaining and reinvesting £2. X is only retaining and reinvesting £1. Y will grow quicker than X. And growth should lead to higher dividends in future years.

Appendix

Appendix A
Depreciation Methods

There are at least ten methods of calculating depreciation. The following are the most commonly used methods.

The fixed instalment method

This is also called the straight-line method.

Example

DB Ltd buy a vehicle costing £20,000 at 1 January, Year 1. The directors decide that the company will use the vehicle for three years, then sell it. They expect that the sale will realise about £2,000. The amount of £2,000 is called the *residual value*.

The calculation of annual depreciation is:

	£
Cost	20,000
Less: residual value	2,000
Total depreciation	18,000

Dividing £18,000 by 3 years gives an annual depreciation charge of £6,000.

The diminishing balance method

Instead of using the straight-line method, the directors of DB Ltd decide to depreciate the vehicle by an amount equal to 50 per cent of the book value at the beginning of the year. Over the three-year life of the vehicle the depreciation charge is calculated as follows:

		£
Year 1	Cost	20,000
	Less: depreciation 50 per cent	10,000
	Book value	10,000
Year 2	Less: depreciation 50 per cent of £10,000	5,000
	Book value	5,000
Year 3	Less: depreciation 50 per cent of £5,000	2,500
	Book value	2,500

The fixed instalment method will arrive at a book value of £2,000 at the end of Year 3. The diminishing balance method will arrive at a book value of £2,500 at the end of Year 3.

But compare the annual amounts of depreciation:

ANNUAL DEPRECIATION

	Straight line £	Diminishing balance £
Year 1	6,000	10,000
Year 3	6,000	2,500

With the straight-line method, the depreciation charge is the same in each year.

With the diminishing balance method, the depreciation charge is high in the early years and small in the later years.

The diminishing balance method is suitable for assets which do, in fact, lose value quickly in the early years. Motor vehicles, computers and electronic equipment tend to fall into this category.

Appendix B
Current Cost Accounting

The object of current cost accounting (CCA) is to show the profit after making provision for the impact of price changes on the funds needed to keep the business going at its present level.

The amount held back from profits (which is transferred to a reserve) is calculated as follows:

1. Depreciation is increased to meet higher replacement costs.
2. 'Cost of sales adjustment'.
   In times of inflation, 'inflation' profits are made simply because the selling price of a stock item has gone up between the time the item was bought and when it was sold.
   The total 'inflation' profit for the past year is calculated at the end of the year, by means of a formula, and is transferred to reserve to help meet the increased cost of holding stocks, resulting from inflation.
3. The increase in debtors (less creditors) and cash balances resulting from inflation is calculated ('monetary working capital adjustment'). The amount of this increase is transferred from profits to reserve.
4. The 'saving' which results because medium-/long-term borrowings are paid off in depreciated money is calculated. This 'saving' (called the 'gearing adjustment') is deducted from items 1-3.

Balance sheet
In the balance sheet, fixed assets are shown at their 'value to the business'. 'Value to the business' is usually taken either as the replacement cost (less depreciation) or the amount which would be realised if the asset was sold off ('net realisable value'). The choice of method depends on whether or not the asset could in fact be replaced.

Deferred Taxation

Tax charge after deducting the full amount of deferred taxation from profits

Trading profit
Depreciation

Profit
Tax *provision* (50 per cent)

After tax profit

Tax charge after deducting from profits the tax actually payable

Trading profit
Depreciation

Profit
Tax *payable*

After tax profit (loss)

Tax assessment
Profit
Less: capital allowance

Taxable profit (or assessed loss)
Tax at 50 per cent

A thought: supposing the 'after tax profit' in years 1-3 of £120,000 had been distributed?

Situation

(a) Annual trading profit over five years *before* depreciation –
£100,000 pa.
(b) In year 1 bought machine for £300,000.
(c) Depreciate machine over five years at £60,000 pa.
(d) Income tax rate 50 per cent.
(e) Depreciation is *not* tax deductible: 'capital allowance' granted in year
1 is equal to 100 per cent of the cost of the machine.

Year 1	Year 2	Year 3	Year 4	Year 5	Total
£	£	£	£	£	£
100,000	100,000	100,000	100,000	100,000	500,000
60,000	60,000	60,000	60,000	60,000	300,000
40,000	40,000	40,000	40,000	40,000	200,000
20,000	20,000	20,000	20,000	20,000	100,000
20,000	20,000	20,000	20,000	20,000	100,000

100,000	100,000	100,000	100,000	100,000	500,000
60,000	60,000	60,000	60,000	60,000	300,000
40,000	40,000	40,000	40,000	40,000	200,000
Nil	Nil	Nil	50,000	50,000	100,000
40,000	40,000	40,000	(10,000)	(10,000)	100,000

100,000	100,000	100,000	100,000	100,000	
300,000	–	–	–	–	
(200,000)	(100,000)	Nil	100,000	100,000	
Nil	Nil	Nil	50,000	50,000	

Appendix D
Marks & Spencer plc

Figures D1 and D2 show the group profit and loss account and balance sheet for Marks & Spencer plc for 1986/87.

An analysis of the Marks & Spencer accounts using the ratios discussed in Chapter 11 then follows.

The balance sheet is set out in a style laid down in the 1981 amendments to the British Companies Act. This style follows a directive of the European Community.

The difference between the 1981 style and the style we have used in this book is that, under the Act, medium-/long-term liabilities are deducted from fixed assets and working capital to give a net worth figure. At the bottom of the balance sheet, the make-up of the net worth (capital) is given.

What we have called medium-/long-term liabilities are described in the 1981 format as 'Creditors: amounts falling due after more than one year'.

Marks & Spencer plc
Consolidated profit and loss account
for the year ended 31 March 1987

	1987 £m	1986 £m
Turnover	4,220.8	3,734.8
Cost of sales	2,915.8	2,666.5
Gross profit	1,305.0	1,068.3
Other expenses	872.9	702.5

Profit on ordinary activities		
before taxation	432.1	365.8
Tax on profit on ordinary activities	156.2	141.3
Profit on ordinary activities		
after taxation	275.9	224.5
Minority interests	(0.1)	2.1
Profit for the financial year	276.0	222.4
Dividends		
Preference shares	0.1	0.1
Ordinary shares:		
Interim of 1.4p per share	37.1	33.0
Final of 3.1p per share	82.3	70.1
	119.5	103.2
Undistributed surplus	156.5	119.2
Earnings per share	10.4p	8.4p

Figure D1

**Marks & Spencer plc
Balance Sheet at 31 March 1987**

	The Group	
	1987 £m	1986 £m
Fixed assets		
Tangible assets:		
Land and buildings	1,322.6	1,243.9
Fixtures, fittings and equipment	274.7	201.4
Assets in course of construction	39.3	16.6
	1,636.6	1,461.9
Investments	–	–
Net assets of financial activities	51.3	18.3
	1,687.9	1,480.2

Current assets		
Stocks	255.4	235.3
Debtors	114.9	102.9
Investments	38.0	75.7
Cash at bank and in hand	58.8	96.6
	467.1	510.5
Current liabilities		
Creditors: amounts falling due within one year	529.9	481.7
Net current assets (excluding financial activities)	(62.8)	28.8
Total assets less current liabilities	1,625.1	1,509.0
Creditors: amounts falling due after more than one year	46.3	46.1
Net assets	1,578.8	1,462.9
Capital and reserves		
Called up share capital	664.8	662.7
Share premium account	13.5	5.8
Revaluation reserve	86.4	84.0
Profit and loss account	814.1	699.9
Shareholders' funds	1,578.8	1,452.4
Minority interests	–	10.5
Total capital employed	1,578.8	1,462.9

Figure D2

Gearing ratios

Equity as a percentage of capital employed

Marks & Spencer describe the group equity of £1,578.8 million as 'total capital employed'. There is no standard definition of the term capital employed, and it can be used to describe either equity or equity plus medium-/long-term liabilities.

We will use the second definition of capital employed, and therefore the capital employed by Marks & Spencer at 31 March 1987 was:

	£m
Equity	1,578.8
Creditors: amounts falling due after more than one year	46.3
Capital employed	1,625.1

£1,578.8 million as a percentage of £1,625.1 is 97.1 per cent (previous year 96.9 per cent). The company is therefore very low geared – outside borrowing is minor. The medium-/long-term liabilities of £46.3 million are mainly mortgage debentures redeemable up to the year 2000 and carrying interest ranging from 5½ per cent to 7¾ per cent per annum.

The medium-/long-term liabilities do not include deferred taxation. The company provides for the deferred taxation on the 'partial allocation' method. As a note to the balance sheet, however, the directors report that there is a contingent liability for deferred taxation of £117.7 million.

This does not include deferred taxation on revalued properties as, in the opinion of the directors, these properties will be retained for use in the business and the likelihood of any taxation liability arising is remote.

(The information about the debentures and deferred tax is taken from the Notes to the balance sheet.)

Interest bearing debt ratio
(Interest bearing debt as a percentage of equity.)

	£m
Interest bearing debt:	
Medium-/long-term liabilities	46.3
Bank loans and overdrafts included in current liabilities (from Notes)	30.5
	76.8

£76.8 million as a percentage of equity £1,578.8 million is 4.9 per cent (last year – 5.6 per cent).

The interest bearing debt is insignificant.

Working capital ratios

Current ratio

Current assets	£m 467.1	= 0.9:1 (last year 1.1:1)
Current liabilities	529.9	

Acid test

Debtors + Investments + Cash = 114.9 + 38.0 + 58.8

Current liabilities

$$= \frac{\substack{£m \\ 211.7}}{529.9}$$

= 0.4:1 (last year 0.6:1)

If we compare these ratios with the 'norms' of 2:1 (current ratio) and 1:1 (acid test), one gets the impression that the company must have working capital and liquidity problems. In fact, at 31 March 1987 the trading part of the group had no working capital – current liabilities exceeded current assets by £62.8 million. (The asset 'net assets of financial activities', however, includes £51.3 million of working capital.) But the financial standing of Marks & Spencer is extremely high. So how are the low ratios explained?

Part of the answer seems to be that much of the current liabilities is made up of items like dividend, taxation, bank loans and overdrafts which will only be cleared some considerable time after the date of the balance sheet. Also, as the group owns unencumbered land and buildings with a book value of £1,322 million, there will be no problem in obtaining short-term finance when needed.

Another factor is the rapid stock turn. The faster the stock turns over, the less stock – and working capital – is needed.

The stock turn can be calculated by dividing average stock (at cost) into cost of sales (this gives the same result as dividing average stock at retail into turnover).

$$\frac{\text{Cost of sales}}{\text{Average stock}} \quad \frac{£2,915.8m}{\frac{1}{2}(£255.4m + £235.3m)} = 11.9 \text{ times}$$

Stock is turning over almost once a month, which is a very high rate considering the wide range of merchandise carried.

Efficiency ratios

Percentage increase in before-tax profits
In the Notes the company gives the before-tax profit for the past five years as shown in Figure D3.

	Before tax profit	Increase over previous year
	£m	%
1987	432.1	18.1
1986	365.8	20.3
1985	304.1	8.9
1984	279.3	16.7
1983	239.3	7.7
1982	222.1	22.6

Figure D3

The average increase, year on year, has been 15.7 per cent. Excellent. (During this period the average annual price inflation in Britain has been about 6 per cent.)

Return on equity (or return on investment)

Profit after tax (£275.9 million) as a percentage of equity (£1,578.8 million): 17.5 per cent (last year 15.3 per cent).

The average return on equity for British businesses in 1986 was approximately 12.5 per cent. Marks & Spencer's return was therefore above average, despite very low gearing. This percentage is influenced by the value put on the land and buildings (see page 100).

Trading profit (before tax and interest) as a percentage of turnover

The Notes tell us that the profit before taxation of £432.1 million, shown in the consolidated profit and loss account, includes a profit on financial activities of £4.8 million. The profit from retailing alone is therefore £427.3 million. The Notes also tell us that, of the turnover of £4,220.8 million, £4,184.2 million is from retailing.

The trading profit as a percentage of turnover from retailing is therefore 10.2 per cent (previous year 10.0 per cent).

One has to compare this percentage with chain stores in the same field. Marks & Spencer retail a wide variety of merchandise, ranging from food to furniture, carrying varying mark-ups, stock turn and operating costs. Comparison with other firms will not be simple.

Trading profit (before tax and interest) as a percentage of total assets

	£m
Total trading assets: fixed	1,636.6
current	467.1
	2,103.7

Trading profit before tax is £427.3 million. Return on total trading assets is therefore 20.3 per cent (previous year 18.8 per cent).

We need to compare this percentage with other firms in the same activity. But the profitability of the assets is influenced by the fact that almost three-quarters of the money invested is in the form of fixed assets – mostly buildings. The profitability of money invested in buildings may be considerably less than that of money invested in current assets – the trading assets. We would need to bear in mind in a comparison with other chain stores. The actual value of the land and buildings is probably greater than the book value. If the land and buildings were shown at true value, this percentage would probably be reduced.

The company has borrowed money through debentures at a maximum interest rate of 7¾ per cent per annum. As the money borrowed is producing a return of 20.3 per cent, the benefits to the company's profitability of this small amount of gearing can be seen.

A Percentage Balance Sheet at 31 March 1987

Liabilities	£m	%	Assets	£m	%
Equity	1,578.8	73.3	Fixed assets		
Medium-/long-term liabilities	46.3	2.1	Land and buildings	1,322.6	61.4
Current liabilities	529.9	24.6	Other	365.3	17.0
			Current assets		
			Stock	255.4	11.9
			Debtors, cash, etc	211.7	9.7
Total liabilities	2,155.0	100.0	Total assets	2,155.0	100.0

Figure D4

Comparison of a percentage balance sheet with other companies in the same field deepens one's knowledge of the company under review. Even without comparison the percentage balance sheet for Marks & Spencer suggests that the company might almost be thought of as a low geared property investment company which runs a retail operation, the retail operation being financed from current liabilities. Historically, the company is a retail operation, but an entrepreneur looking at the balance sheet may see it in a different light.

The United Kingdom land and buildings were last revalued in 1982. An up-to-date revaluation of the land and buildings would probably increase the assets, and equity, substantially.

Debt repayment ratio

(This is medium-/long-term debt divided by typical annual profits retention.)

As the retention in 1986 was £119.2 million and in 1987 £156.5 million, a reasonably 'typical' retention would be £140 million.

Dividing £140 million into the medium-/long-term debt of £46.3 million gives 0.33. In other words, the company is retaining enough profit to pay off, if so desired, the medium-/long-term debt in 33 per cent of a year – about four months. This is another reflection of the company's low gearing.

Appendix E
Statement of Source and Application of Funds

This statement is usually published together with the profit and loss account and balance sheet of a company. It is to show the funds received by the company *in the year up to the date of the balance sheet*, and how those funds were used.

The figures for the statement are found by comparing the balance sheet at the end of the year with the previous balance sheet. Figure E1 shows a simplified comparison.

ML Limited
Balance Sheet

	At 31 December 1998	At 31 December 1999	Change
	£	£	£
Share capital	500	600	+100
Retained profit	300	375	+ 75
Equity	800	975	+175
Loans	90	80	- 10
Capital employed	890	1,055	+165

Employment of capital

Fixed assets

Cost	500	540	+ 40
Less: provision for depreciation	160	180	+ 20
Book value	340	360	+ 20
Working capital	550	695	+145
	890	1,055	+165

Figure E1

The statement can be set out in one of two ways, using the *plus* and *minus* figures in the 'change' column.

Method 1

Source and application of funds for the year ended 31 December 1999 (Figure E2).

Sources of funds	£
Increase in share capital	100
Increase in retained profit	75
Increase in depreciation provision	20
	195

Application of funds	
Repayment of loan	10
Cost of additional fixed assets	40
Increase in working capital	145
	195

Figure E2

The increase in the depreciation provision is a source because the increase is profit set aside to meet the cost of replacement of fixed assets. The increase is, in effect, a further retention of profit in the business.

Method 2

		£
Working capital at 31 December 1998:		550
Add: sources of funds during the year		
• increase in share capital		100
• increase in retained profit		75
• increase in depreciation provision		20
		745
Less: application of funds:		
• repayment of loan	10	
• cost of additional fixed assets	40	50
Working capital at 31 December 1999		695

Figure E3

The statement of sources and application of funds is useful because it highlights:

- The change in the amount of working capital;
- How the money spent on the purchase of fixed assets compares with the depreciation for the year – Note, however, that the purchases will include both replacements and additions;
- Whether the amount of debt repayment (less new borrowings) is covered by the profit retained for the year;
- How the amount of any net additional borrowing compares with any increase in equity. Is the company becoming more highly geared?

Preparing a combined statement covering the past five years will give a good insight into a company's finances.

Glossary

accounts payable Creditors.

accounts receivable Debtors.

acid test Comparison of 'quick assets' (cash and debtors) with a company's current liabilities. A rough yardstick is that quick assets should be at least equalto the current liabilities.

amortisation Another word for depreciation or writing off an asset.

appropriation account A statement published together with the balance sheet of a company which shows how the net profit for the year is distributed or 'appropriated'. The appropriations are income tax, preference dividends, transfer to general reserve and ordinary dividends.

Articles of Association The part of a company's constitution which deals with the inner working sof the company – how meetings are called and conducted, the appointment of company officers, etc.

asset stripping The process whereby a holding company acquires control of a subsidiary for a price which is less than the realisation value of the assets. The holding company then causes the subsidiary to sell off its assets, creating profits in the subsidiary. The resulting cash is drawn out of the subsidiary by the holding company as dividends, loans, etc.

associated companies A company in which the investing company holds at least 20 per cent of the shares and influences the management of the company, but which is not a subsidiary (*qv*) of the investing company.

attributable profit The net profit of a company or group including its proportion of the profits of subsidiary and associated companies.

authorised share capital The maximum number of shares a company may issue,as set out in the company's Memorandum of Association. The share capital *issued* is often *less* than the authorised share capital. The authorised share capital (also called nominal share capital; *qv*) puts a limit on the number of shares the directors may issue. The authorised share capital can only be increased by a resolution of the shareholders.

balance sheet A list of the assets, liabilities, and equity (*qv*) of a business at a point in time.

bed and breakfasting An investor holds shares which have fallen in value. He wishes to retain the shares, but uses the loss to reduce his liability for capital gains tax. Therefore, near the end of the tax year, he sells the shares and buys them back on the same day. This creastes a tax deductible loss.

bonus shares Shares issued free to existing ordinary shareholders. The issue is financed out of the retained profits of the company. Also called a 'scrip issue'.

book value The cost of a fixed asset less the accumulated depreciation provision (see **depreciation**). The book value may be greater or smaller than the realisable value. Realisable value depends on the circumstances under which an asset is sold.

capital The value of the owner's investment in a business.

capital employed There are various definitions, but usually capital employed is regarded as equity plus medium-/long-term liabilities.

capital expenditure Money spent on fixed assets.

capital profits Profits made on the sale of assets. Contrast this with revenue profits which result from the business's trading or other regular operations.

capital reserve An addition to the equity resulting from an increase in the value of assets, especially land and buildings. Until the revalued asset is sold and becomes cash, the amount of capital reserve is not normally available for distribution as a dividend (UK – revaluation reserve). The capital reserve of a company will also include the amount of any share premiums (*qv*) received. Capital reserves are regarded as non-distributable.

capitalisation issue A rights issue (*qv*). Also sometimes used to mean a bonus issue.

cash flow Balance sheet analysts use this tern to mean the retained profits of a company for the year, plus the depreciation for the year.

cash flow budget A forecast, prepared by management, of the estimated balances of cash at bank at the end of each month for the next year.

circulating capital Same as current assets (*qv*).

consistency concept An accounting rule that the methods used in working out profit are the same in each year.

consolidated balance sheet A combined balance sheet for a holding company and all its subsidiaries prepared by adding together all the group's assets and liabilities.

contingent liability A liability which may never crystallise, such as a guarantee given by a company on another company's overdraft. Contingent liabilities are shown as a note to the balance sheet.

current assets Assets which will become cash within one year of the balance sheet date. Normally trading stocks, debtors and cash.

current cost accounting An alternative method of preparing a balance sheet as compared with the usual 'historical cost' method. In the CCA balance sheet assets are usually shown at replacement costs. Profit is set aside in a reserve to finance the extra costs of operating which have resulted from inflation. CCA is not popular, and is subject to much debate. It can drastically reduce distributable profits.

current liabilities Liabilities repayable within one year of balance sheet date; normally creditors and overdraft.

current ratio A comparison of current assets with current liabilities. Traditionally, current assets should be about twice the amount of current liabilities. Then the business will be assumed to have sufficient working capital. But a well managed company can often operate with a current ratio of far less than 2:1.

debentures A loan made to a limited company, evidenced by debenture certificates. The certificates are usually transferrable.

deferred shares Also called founders' shares, sometimes issued to the promoters of a company or the previous owner of a business now owned by the company. Deferred shares only receive a dividend after the ordinary shares have received an agreed minimum dividend.

deferred taxation This is taxation on current profits, but payable only in future years. The main cause of this deferral is that many countries allow fixed assets to be deducted from taxable profits at a faster rate than the same assets are depreciated in the company's books. (This is called a 'timing difference'.) As a result the profit shown on the company's tax return is lower than the profit (after depreciation) shown in the balance sheet, and the tax payable is proportionately lower. But once the assets have been fully claimed against tax, the profit on the tax return will be higher than in the balance sheet. The tax burden is proportionately low in the first years, higher later; therefore the full burden of tax is 'deferred'. Some companies set aside from profits the amount of deferred tax, as a provision. This evens out the yearly tax burden. Most companies, however, only show the deferred tax as a note to the balance sheet.

depreciation The process of setting aside profit, each year, to finance the replacement of fixed assets as they wear out or become obsolete ('depreciate'). The cumulative amount of profit set aside appears in the balance sheet under the title 'depreciation provision'. See also **book value.**

earnings per share The after-tax profit of a company for the year, divided by the number of ordinary shares in issue. Usually only a portion of the earnings (often about half) will be paid as a dividend on the shares.

equity Same as capital (*qv*).

FIFO Acronym for 'first in, first out'. A way of valuing trading stock, on the assumption that the first stock item received was the first to be sold. Consequently, stock is valued at the cost price of the last consignments received. See page 39.

financial bath The process whereby the new management of an ailing company writes down all the assets to realistic values, and makes provisions for all possible liabilities. This is done in the first year and results in greatly reduced profit, or even a loss for the year, but leaves a 'clean' balance sheet.

fixed assets The permanent equipment of a business – buildings, vehicles, machinery, furniture, etc.

floating charge A mortgage deed signed by a business borrowing money which pledges moveable assets such as equipment, stock, debtors, as security for repayment of the loan.

gearing The proportion of borrowing to equity. If equity is low, borrowings high, the company is said to be 'highly geared'.

general reserve Profit set aside, and added to equity, usually because it is not practicable to distribute the profit as a dividend. This is because the profit has been used to finance business expansion, or the costs of inflation, and is not available as cash.

going concern basis Normally balance sheets show asset values on the assumption that the business will carry on. This is called the 'going concern basis'. The alternative, used in exceptional circumstances, is to show the assets at their break-up value, which will normally be far less than going concern values.

goodwill The value of a business over and above the value of its assets. Goodwill represents the value of a business's reputation, know-how, franchises, and so on. Although there are formulas for calculating goodwill, the true value is the amount a buyer is willing to pay for the business, in excess of the value of its assets.

gross dividend The amount of a dividend *before* deducting tax. In the UK, dividends are paid net, but the amount is then 'grossed up', using the standard rate of tax, to give the gross dividend amount for tax return and statistical purposes (called the 'imputation method').

gross profit The difference between the sales for a period, and the cost of the goods sold. Operating expenses and overheads are then deducted from the gross profit, leaving the net profit or net loss for the period.

group accounts See **consolidated balance sheet**

historical accounting This is the normal accounting system, in which assets are shown in the books as what they cost, less depreciation. In recent decades, however, mainly due to inflation, it has become common to revalue upwards assets like land and buildings, thus departing from historical cost. Current cost accounting (*qv*) is a major departure from historical cost accounting.

holding company The 'parent' company of a group, which holds a majority shareholding in, or otherwise controls, its subsidiary companies.

incorporation The legal process of forming a business into a limited liability company.

inflation accounting See **current cost accounting.**

inventory Same as trading stock.

investment trusts Despite the name, these are quoted limited companies, which invest their resources in shares. The public invest in investment trusts by buying the trust's shares on the stock market. The price the shareholder receives when he sells his shares in the truse therefore depends on the current stock market price of the trust's shares – which is often less than the value of the trust's investments. Contrast this with unit trusts (*qv*). Unlike unit trusts, investment trusts can borrow, and therefore enjoy the benefits of gearing (*qv*).

joint stock company Same as limited liability company (*qv*).

leverage See **gearing.**

LIFO Last in, first out, see page 39.

limited liability company A separate legal entity formed in terms of the Companies Act. The owners of a company are the shareholders. The liability of the shareholders for the company's unpaid debts is limited to the amount they have invested, or promised to invest, in shares.

liquid assets Cash and assets which can be turned into cash in a few hours – like quoted investments, deposits, etc.

liquidity ratio See **acid test.**

market capitalisation The quoted price of a company's shares multiplied by the number of shares in issue.

matching concept An accounting rule that in calculating the profit for the year the expenses and the earnings must both be for a period of 365 days.

materiality An accounting rule that financial statements should disclose all items which are large enough to affect materially the evaluation of profit or net worth.

Memorandum of Association Part of the constitution of a limited company. The Memorandum states the name of the company, the company's objectives and gives details of the authorised share capital (*qv*).

minority shareholders The shareholders who hold the minority of shares in a subsidiary company, the majority of shares being held by the holding company. The proportion of equity belonging to the minority shareholders is shown separately in the consolidated balance sheet.

mortgage debentures A debenture loan secured by a mortgage over the assets of the company.

net dividend See **gross dividend.**
net profit See **gross profit.**
nominal share capital See **authorised share capital.**
nominal value of a share The face value, printed on the share certificate, eg £1, 50 pence, 25 pence, etc.

ordinary shares These shares normally carry a vote, so the ordinary shareholders control a company. The profits of the company, after payment of any preference dividend, belong to the ordinary shareholders who normally receive part of the profits as the annual dividend. The amount of the dividend varies with the size of the annual profit.

paid up capital The total nominal value of all shares issued by a company and paid for.

par value The nominal value of a share (*qv*).

PE ratio Short for price/earnings ratio. The PE ratio is calculated by dividing the market price by the annual earnings (ie after-tax profit) per share.

plc Abbreviation for public limited company – used in the UK.

pre-emption rights If provided for in the Articles of Association, existing shareholders have a right to subscribe to new shares issued by the company, ahead of new shareholders.

preference shares These shares carry a fixed dividend and usually have no vote.the payment of a preference dividend takes priority over the dividend on ordinary shares. If the company is wound up, the preference shareholders take priority over ordinary shareholders in the repayment of their investment.

private company A company in which the number of shareholders is restricted. The shares of a private company may not be traded in. In return for these restrictions, private companies are exempted from certain legal requirements. In some countries the abbreviation PVT or PTY is included in the name of the company.

profit and loss account An annual statement of income, less expenses, giving the net profit for the year.

provision Profit set aside, and retained in the company, to meet possible or probable future commitments or losses resulting from the year's activities. Examples are a provision for doubtful debts, a provision for the replacement of fixed assets (depreciation provision), a provision for taxation, etc.

prudence concept An accounting rule that profits should not be anticipated but should only be shown in the profit statement in the year in which the transaction creating the profit takes place. But, on the other hand, the profit statement must include provision for all expenses and losses relating to the year, even if the expenses or losses may only arise in future years.

public company A company which may have an unlimited number of shareholders, and whose shares may be offered to the public. The shares in 'quoted' public companies are traded on a Stock Exchange.

quoted shares Shares traded on the Stock Exchange, so that there is a daily price 'quoted' in the financial press.

reserves Profits retained in the business to finance general growth and expansion; contrast with provision. See also **revenue reserves** and **capital reserve**.

return on equity After-tax profit for the year expressed as a percentage of equity.

return on investment Same as return on equity (*qv*).

revaluation reserve See **capital reserve**.

revenue expenditure Money spend on the operating expenses of a business.

revenue reserves Distributable profit set aside by the company to finance expansion or strengthen the business.

rights issue Existing shareholders are invited to buy further shares in their company, proportionate to their existing holdings. The 'rights issue' is normally offered at a price less than the current market price. If a shareholder does not with to buy the additional shares, he may sell his 'rights' to someone else.

scrip issue See **bonus shares.**

secret reserves By deliberately writing down assets to unrealistically low levels, and by making provisions which are much greater than justified, a company will understate its net worth. The amount of the understatement is caled a secret or hidden reserve.

share premium Shares may be issued by a company at a price greater than the nominal value. The extra amount is called a share premium and is shown as part of the equity, under the heading capital reserve.

stocks As in stocks and shares, instead of issuing shares in units with a nominal value, a company's issued capital is described as 'stock' and the stock is issued in fractions. You might, for instance, buy stock in a company with a nominal value of £765.67. (In the UK, the term usually means loan stock.)

subsidiary company See **holding company.**

takeover The act of one company taking over control of another company by acquiring a majority shareholding.

turnover A business's sales for a year.

unit trusts The public buy units in the trust, and the trustees invest the money in shares. The unit holder will receive a dividend on his units and also hopes the units will increase in value. At any time the unit holder can sell his units back to the trust. The price the unit holder will then receive is based on the present value of the trust's investments.

wasting asset An asset which is exhausted in the business operation, like the cost of a mining claim.

working capital The cushion of money a business uses to trade with. Calculated by deducting current liabilities from current assets.

Index

Further Reading from Kogan Page

Finance and Accounts for Managers, Desmond Goch, 1986
Financial Management for the Small Business, 2nd edition, Colin Barrow, 1988
Funding Your Business, Kenneth Winckles, 1988
Making Corporate Reports Valuable, ed Peter McMonnies, 1988
Management Accounting for the Company Executive, T M Walker, 1987
A Practical Guide to Creative Accounting, Michael Jameson, 1987
Understand Your Accounts, 2nd edition, A St John Price, 1986

Kogan Page publish an extensive list of books for professional managers and small and medium-sized businesses. Details are available from 120 Pentonville Road, London N1 9JN.